PAST AWAYS™

PAST AWAYS™

FACEDOWN IN THE TIMESTREAM

URSULA

HERB

MARGE

SCRIPT
MATT KINDT

ART
SCOTT KOLINS

COLORS, "PAST IS PROLOGUE"
AND CHAPTERS 1–5, 7–9
BILL CRABTREE

COLORS, CHAPTER 6
WES DZIOBA

LETTERS
ROB LEIGH

COVER ART AND CHAPTER BREAKS
SCOTT KOLINS

TRAVELOGUE ART
MATT KINDT

DARK HORSE BOOKS

PRESIDENT AND PUBLISHER
MIKE RICHARDSON

COLLECTION EDITOR
DANIEL CHABON

EDITORS
BRENDAN WRIGHT AND DANIEL CHABON

ASSISTANT EDITORS
IAN TUCKER AND CARDNER CLARK

DESIGNER
JIMMY PRESLER

DIGITAL ART TECHNICIAN
JASON RICKERD

Published by Dark Horse Books
A division of Dark Horse Comics, Inc.
10956 SE Main Street
Milwaukie, OR 97222

First edition: July 2016
ISBN 978-1-61655-792-8

10 9 8 7 6 5 4 3 2 1
Printed in China

International Licensing: (503) 905-2377
Comic Shop Locator Service: (888) 266-4226

Past Aways: Facedown in the Timestream

This volume collects *Past Aways* #1—#9 and the short story "Past Is Prologue" from *Dark Horse Presents* #6.

Library of Congress Cataloging-in-Publication Data
Names: Kindt, Matt, author, illustrator. | Kolins, Scott, illustrator. | Crabtree, Bill (Comic book colorist) illustrator. | Dzioba, Wes, illustrator. | Leigh, Rob, illustrator.
Title: Past aways : facedown in the timestream / script, Matt Kindt ; art, Scott Kolins ; colors, "Past Is Prologue" and chapters 1-5, 7-9, Bill Crabtree ; colors, chapter 6, Wes Dzioba ; letters, Rob Leigh ; cover art and chapter breaks, Scott Kolins ; travelogue art, Matt Kindt.
Description: First edition. | Milwaukie, OR : Dark Horse Books, 2016. | "This volume collects Past Aways #1-#9 and the short story "Past Is Prologue" from Dark Horse Presents #6."
Identifiers: LCCN 2016004338 | ISBN 9781616557928
Classification: LCC PN6727.K54 P37 2016 | DDC 741.5/973--dc23
LC record available at http://lccn.loc.gov/2016004338

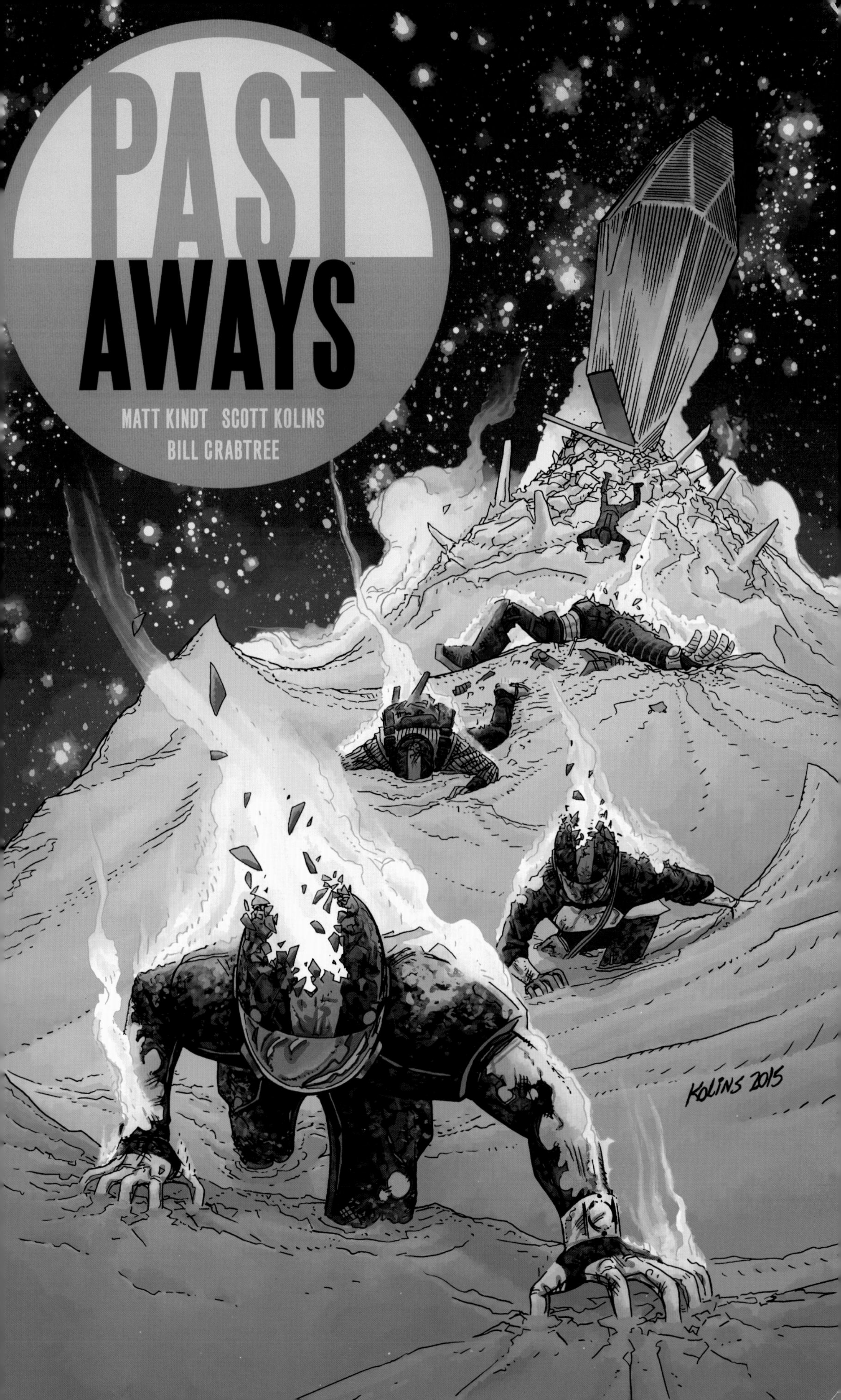
PAST AWAYS™
MATT KINDT SCOTT KOLINS
BILL CRABTREE
KOLINS 2015

Time travel is a tricky thing.

That should go without saying.
CRASH

Landings, on the other hand...

Those are usually routine.

The chronobeacon, made of ultralight derivativium alloys, is a complex perpetual-motion homing mechanism designed to withstand time and space travel. It is an essential safety feature on every transspace vehicle currently in production.

☐ The 100x suit is designed to withstand millions of pounds of pressure, vacuums, and intense heat. Several recent models have undergone a recall due to a flaw in the heat-sync system that, in rare instances, causes "catastrophic failure" (i.e., bursts into flames).

...is loud...

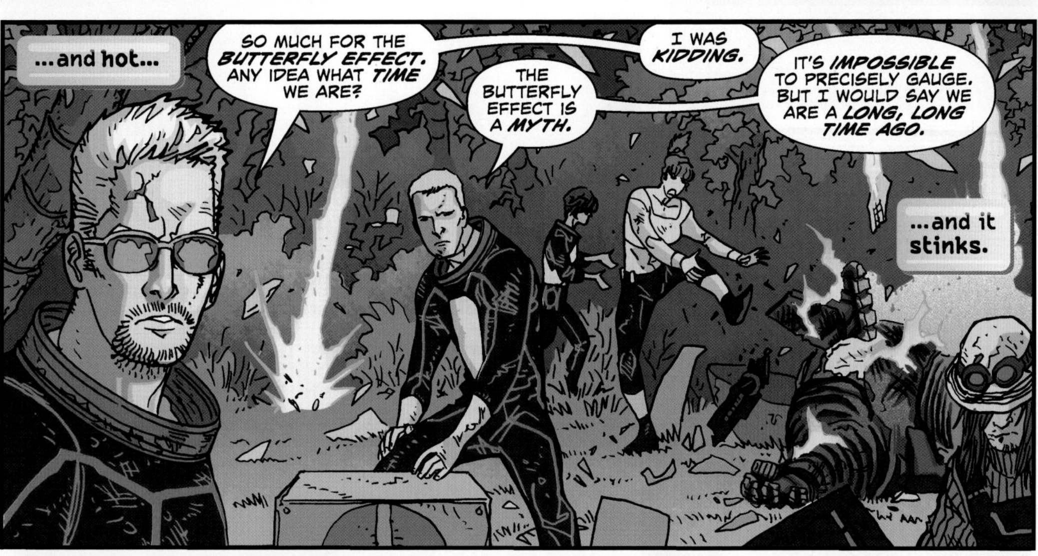

...and hot...
SO MUCH FOR THE BUTTERFLY EFFECT. ANY IDEA WHAT TIME WE ARE?
THE BUTTERFLY EFFECT IS A MYTH.
I WAS KIDDING.
IT'S IMPOSSIBLE TO PRECISELY GAUGE. BUT I WOULD SAY WE ARE A LONG, LONG TIME AGO.
...and it stinks.

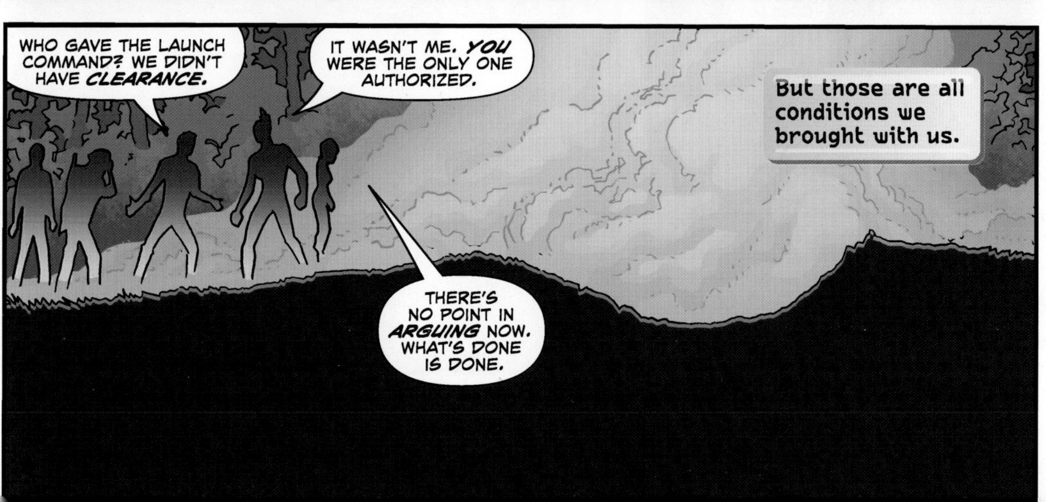

WHO GAVE THE LAUNCH COMMAND? WE DIDN'T HAVE CLEARANCE.
IT WASN'T ME. YOU WERE THE ONLY ONE AUTHORIZED.
But those are all conditions we brought with us.
THERE'S NO POINT IN ARGUING NOW. WHAT'S DONE IS DONE.

THE ***AUTO-NOCS*** SHOULD BE KICKING IN TO YOUR SYSTEM. IF THERE'S ANY ***PREHISTORIC PATHOGEN*** FLOATING AROUND THEY SHOULD HELP YOU ***FIGHT*** IT.

IF YOU START FEELING ***SICK,*** LET ME KNOW.

It is a beautiful land, unspoiled. Untouched.

My mission is a **simple** one. Travel to prehistory and **document** everything.

Every member of the team has a unique **task**, each selected to dovetail with each **personality**.

HAS ANYONE SCANNED THE AREA FOR LIFE?

ASK ***PHIL.*** THAT ISN'T ***MY JOB.***

YEAH. APPARENTLY YOUR JOB IS ***CATCHING FIRE*** AND RUINING OUR ***ONLY*** 100X SUIT.

Autoinoculators are loaded with every known serum, cure, and preventative tincture. Encased in a subcutaneous dispenser, they constantly deliver the correct dosages as they scan the environment for air- and blood-borne pathogens.

PHIL.

WHAT ARE YOU DOING *UP THERE?*

OUR SHIP LEFT A TRAIL OF DEBRIS. WE'LL FOLLOW THE TRAIL AND PICK UP AS MANY PIECES AS WE CAN SALVAGE.
AND HOPE TO CORE WE CAN FIND THE CHRONOBEACON.
ARE WE GOING TO GET BACK?
IF WE CAN FIND THE CHRONOBEACON, THEY CAN JUST SEND US A RETRIEVAL POD.
HERB? ARE YOUR MESSAGES GETTING THROUGH?
IMPOSSIBLE TO TELL, ARTHUR. I'VE BEEN SENDING A STEADY STREAM OF MESSAGES SINCE WE LANDED, WITH NO REPLY.

I'VE FOUND IT.

THE CHRONO-BEACON?

YES, BUT LOOK...

WHAT DID IT LAND ON?

SOME KIND OF PATH...?

Our mission was supposed to last a total of thirty-six Earth hours.

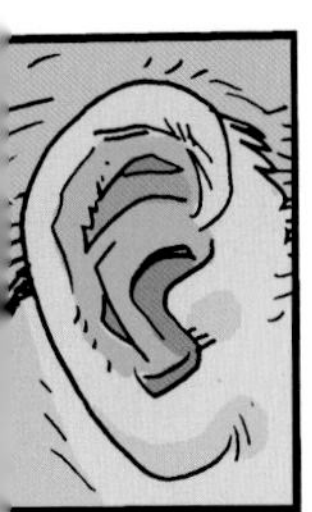

WHAT'S THAT NOISE?
THE BEACON...!
We were to simply gather samples...

WE'VE GOT TO GET THE BEACON OUT OF THE WAY!
...make recordings...
KGANT

...and observe.

Nearly twenty-four hours have gone by...

And I'm afraid...

☐ Four-wheeled, ground-based transportation that runs on fossil fuel. Limited range and durability.

...for all of us.
Margaret: The philosophical head of the team. A tough exterior, but...even harder inside.
IT WAS MEANT TO BE. NO POINT IN CRYING. PREDESTINED, LIKE I TOLD ALL OF YOU.
Ursula: The artist and poet and the heart of our team. Her personality perfect for keeping harmony between us all.
THIS WAS A TRAGEDY, MARGARET...
Arthur: Our fearless leader Possessing an indestructible spirit and tactical genius.
WE BETTE GET THE HELL OUT HERE.
Philip: The perfect human specimen. He's seen more of the universe than the rest of us combined. His knowledge is fathomless.
WE'RE NEVER GOING TO GET BACK HOME.
We've just begun.

PAST AWAYS
MATT KINDT SCOTT KOLINS
BILL CRABTREE
Bipolar weapons specialist. Thinks leader is an a**hole.
Emotionally detached documentarian and technophile.
Team leader. Believes math and science have an answer for everything. Also believes everyone loves him.
Soul and conscience of the team. Secretly wishes she were dead.
Heartless bastard who unfortunately holds the key to everyone's survival.
KOLINS 2016

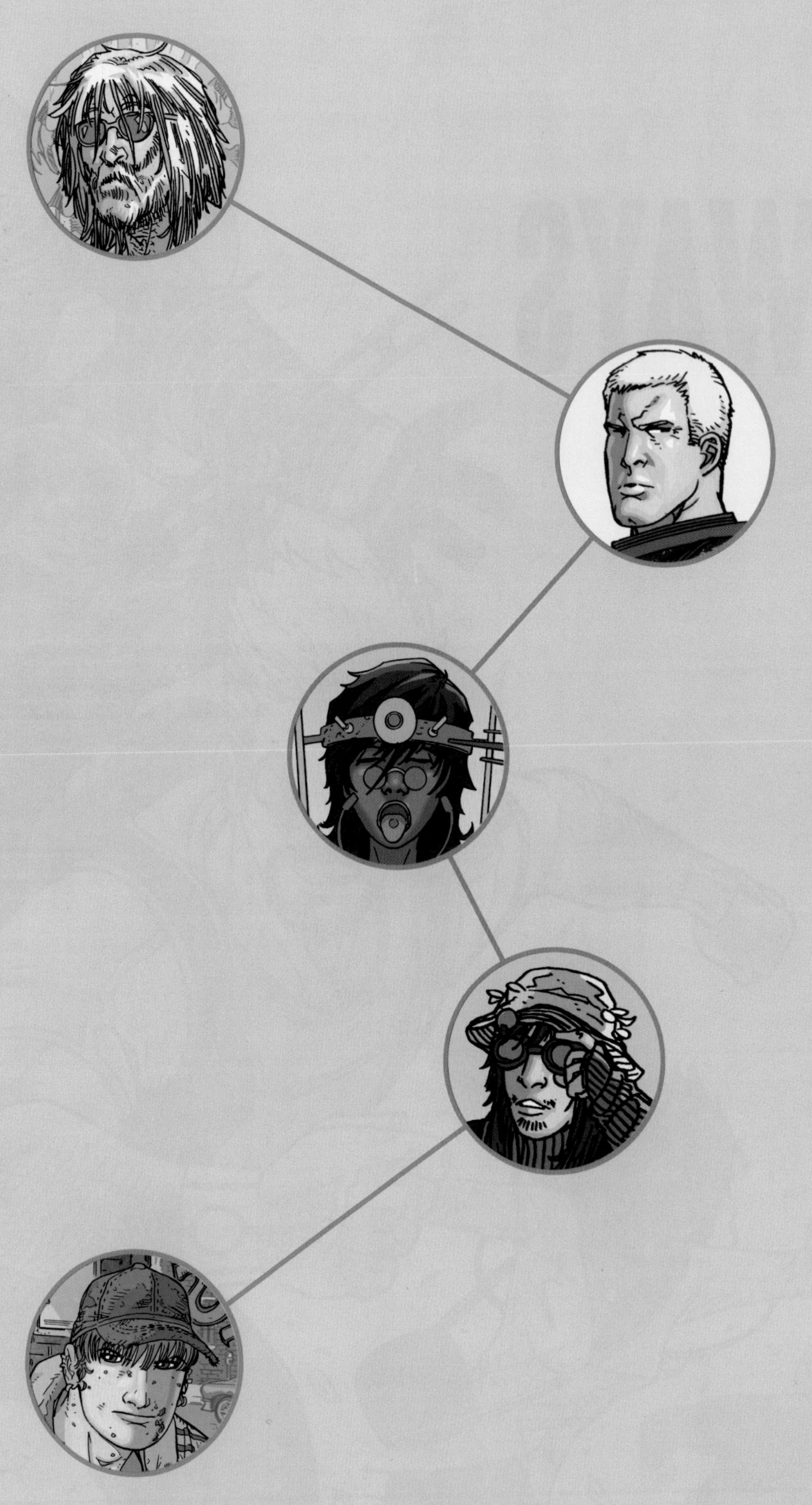

Something strange happened in Greece today.
It was a catalyst.
SCREEEECH
Something unexpected.

Something unexplained.
Something this world has never seen before.
Something that hasn't been seen for thousands of years.
SCRAAHHHHG
Primitive cellular device with basic features that do little more than distract the user from life-threatening, real-world events.

The world watches.
HA HA HA HA HAHA HA HA HA HA HA HA HAH
It is transfixed.
Huh? AH... AHHH!
SKSHHH
They don't realize what they are seeing.
OHMYGOD! GETITOFF! AHHHH!
AHHHHH!
They are witnessing a singular event.
Something beautiful.
Something...

□ Chronohelmet with crimson tint that filters multiple-timeline light sources simultaneously to minimize chronoheadaches. Also impact resistant.

INITIAL REPORTS INDICATED A POSSIBLE TERRORIST ATTACK AND THE POTENTIAL DETONATION OF A "DIRTY BOMB."

BUT MORE RECENT EYEWITNESS ACCOUNTS PAINT QUITE A DIFFERENT PICTURE.
NDEET
NDEET

SEVERAL UNCONFIRMED REPORTS ARE CLAIMING THAT A DINOSAUR HAS BEEN SIGHTED ON THE SCENE.

WHILE MANY BELIEVE THE DISTURBANCE TO BE A HOAX...
Reuniting the team seems impossible at this point, unless a catalyst can be introduced to instigate a reunion organically.

I hope that my predictions prove accurate, and--
MY GOD--!
...THE RESPONSE BY GREECE'S HELLENIC ARMED FORCES HAS BEEN VERY REAL.
IT'S HAPPENED!
Adaptable virtual-reality screen with fluid sound/image progression. Originally designed for extended deep-space missions, but ideal for combating claustrophobia and depression.

...hasn't realized what's happened yet.
I HOPE THIS *WORKS,* HERB...

They are still drifting from moment to moment. Oblivious to the monumental nature of the day that just happened.

I'M SO TIRED...

Huh.

☐ Assisted-suicide device with brain-scanning abilities, allowing it to customize its attack on a subject's brain patterns in a way that induces euphoria, followed by death.

THAT *IS* ODD.
HERE IT GOES. I'LL SEE YOU ON THE OTHER SIDE. JUST GOING TO END IT ALL.
I THINK THIS IS IT! IT'S ***HAPPENING!***
DAMMIT, HERB! ***WHAT?!*** WHAT IS IT?!
THERE'S BEEN SOME KIND OF EVENT...A SINGULARITY. BUT IT'S ***NOT*** SINGULAR! AND THAT'S WHAT MAKES IT SO AMAZING!
sigh

☐ 6-D quintuplifocal lenses capable of layering multiple realities into a hybrid approximating the most accepted reality in existence--all still theoretical and in the testing stages.

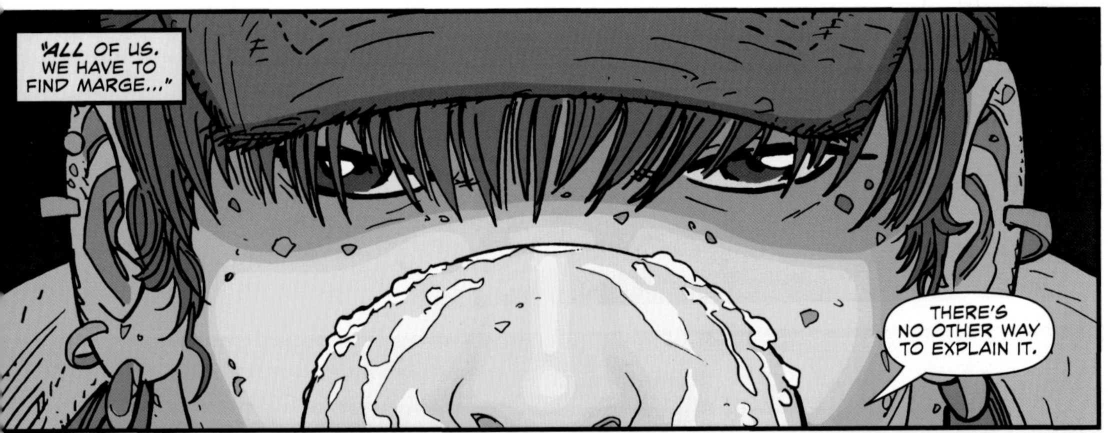
"ALL OF US. WE HAVE TO FIND MARGE..."
THERE'S NO OTHER WAY TO EXPLAIN IT.

THAT'S NOT NECESSARILY RIGHT. THEY'VE STUDIED CHIMPANZEES THAT DISPLAY EMPATHY AND A SENSE OF REGRET.
NOT TRUE. WE PROJECT OUR THOUGHTS AND FEELINGS ONTO OTHER ANIMALS. BECAUSE WE'RE DESPERATE NOT TO BE ALONE IN THIS UNIVERSE. TRUST ME. I'VE SEEN A LOT MORE THAN YOU EVER WILL IN YOUR LIFETIME.
THE SPARK OF COMPASSION WE ALL SHARE...

...WHERE DOES IT COME FROM IF IT ISN'T A PRODUCT OF THE DIVINE?
I DON'T KNOW, LADY, BUT I THINK I CAN GIVE YOU A LITTLE PIECE OF THE DIVINE IF YOU--
BACK--

YOU'RE ALL FOOLS.

KACHAK
OHHHH...
MARGE! GET OUT OF HERE!
I TOLD YOU YOUR NUTTY OPINIONS AREN'T WELCOME HERE!

BOOM

OOPS... DAMMIT...

YOU *STUPID*--!
KCHT

KKSHH

DON'T BE ANGRY.

BE *ENLIGHTENED.*
...UPDATE FROM ATHENS...

Mount Etna, Italy.
PHIL!
HAVE YOU SEEN THE NEWS?

THIS IS IT. WHAT I WAS TALKING ABOUT. IT'S HAPPENED HERE ON EARTH FINALLY.

PHIL-- NO!

NNNF!

YOU'RE JUST... WASTING TIME!

Tritipped darts with a series of lethal explosive-acid payloads, each designed to seek specific DNA targets and kill instantly.

DO WE HAVE TO DO THIS *EVERY TIME,* PHIL?

DÉTENTE, AS ALWAYS. MISSED EVERY VITAL ORGAN. PAINFUL, BUT MERELY...ANNOYING. YOU KNOW I *CAN'T* BE KILLED. JUST LIKE YOU *CAN'T.* OR *ANY* OF US, ARTHUR.

BUT YOU MIGHT WANT TO PULL OUT THE *POISON QUILL* I JAMMED INTO YOUR SHOULDER. *JUST IN CASE.*

I'LL BE *DAMNED.* GOT STUCK IN A *FOLD* OF MY SUIT.
SEE? THIS IS WHY WE NEED YOU BACK.

☐ Quill containing custom poisons derived from rare Martian metals

One hour later...

I SAW THE *REPORTS* AND ASSUMED YOU'D COME TO GET ME.
WHAT'S WITH THE *VOLCANO STUDY?* ANYTHING I NEED TO KNOW ABOUT?
...
I *SEE.*
ANYWAY, I *KNEW* THIS DAY WOULD ARRIVE.

LET'S JUST GET *IN* AND *OUT.* MY WHIRLYBIRD WILL *JAM* ALL PRESENT-DAY ELECTRONICS FOR THE DURATION SO WE CAN MOVE IN WITHOUT BEING *RECORDED.*

LET'S TAKE IT *ALIVE.*

SCRAAAHHW
ART, IF YOU'RE RIGHT AND THIS CREATURE IS FROM THE FUTURE, IT CAN'T BE KILLED. YOU'VE BEEN ***WRONG*** BEFORE.

JUST BE ***CAREFUL.*** THE THING HAS PROJECTILE SPORES THAT CAN BURN THROUGH ANYTHING, INCLUDING YOU...

HSSS

I'LL BE DAMNED. IT'S GOT THEM COMING OUT ***BOTH*** ENDS.

DON'T WORRY, ART.
I'LL TRY NOT TO ***DAMAGE*** IT.

I'VE GOT *HOLD* OF THE ACID-SPORE SACK. CONSIDER IT *NEUTRALIZED.*
Uh... *YEAH.*

I'VE GOT A *CALMING CUBE* IN THE COPTER. LET'S GO.
The Athens event was the catalyst.

Nothing would be the same again. Or should I say, "Nothing had been the same for the first time"?
Either way, time travel is problematic, to say the least.

It has been over a year since the team was last whole.

Ursula and I clung together in Los Angeles. The rest of them scattered to the wind.

To be honest, I think we had all given up hope.
AMBIEN
TAKE ONE PILL
BY MOUTH
AT BEDTIME

Even me.

But now we have concrete **evidence**. There is a **link** to the future.

There is reason to send our progress reports and travel journals. Perhaps **someone** is reading all of this.

□ Trillium alloy designed to send and receive radio signals.

So let me start again.

This is a record of what life was like in the twenty-first century.

Everyday existence is **crude**. It is full of conflict, egos, discomfort, and irreconcilably opposing views on virtually every topic.

To put it bluntly, living here is a **struggle**. It is so **very** different than what the **history blasts** taught us.

But today has brought renewed hope.

But today has brought renewed hope.
Hope that our message is being received. I have once again taken up my post as team documentarian.

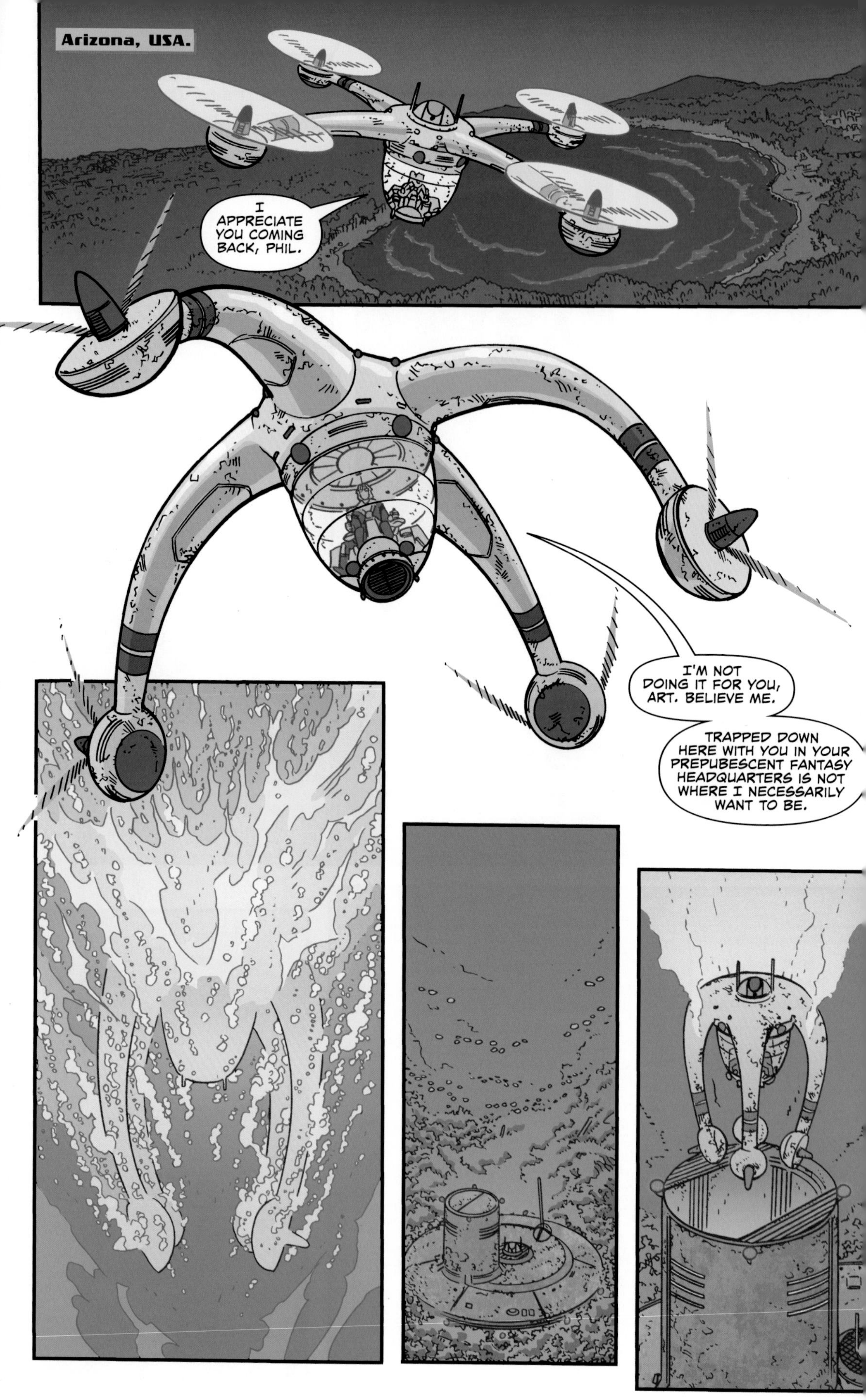
Arizona, USA.
I APPRECIATE YOU COMING BACK, PHIL.
I'M NOT DOING IT FOR YOU, ART. BELIEVE ME.
TRAPPED DOWN HERE WITH YOU IN YOUR PREPUBESCENT FANTASY HEADQUARTERS IS NOT WHERE I NECESSARILY WANT TO BE.

I SEE YOU'VE MAINTAINED THE HEADQUARTERS.
WELL, YEAH. IT'S A LITTLE BIT OF A MESS, BUT I NEVER GAVE UP HOPE, PHIL.
THIS DOESN'T CHANGE ANYTHING BETWEEN US, ART. I WON'T EVER LET YOU KILL ME.
PHIL... COME ON. THIS MEANS I MIGHT NOT *HAVE TO* KILL YOU.

I *WASN'T* GOING TO KILL YOU, ANYWAY.
YOU WOULD HAVE. YOU'LL STILL TRY.
COME ON... YOU'RE RUINING THE MOMENT HERE.

THIS IS IT. I'M CALLING THEM ALL BACK.
My hope is that Art and Phil can resolve their differences.

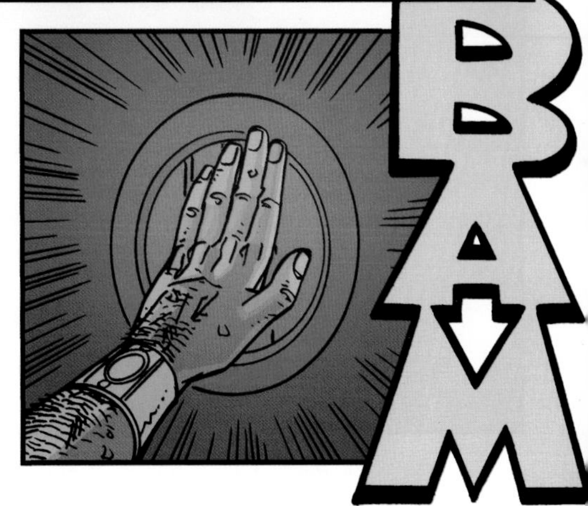
BAM

My **hope** is that Ursula will continue to be our anchor. Once again, keeping us all grounded.

My **hope** is that Marge can be reined in.

My **hope** is that I, Herbert June, will be able to keep sending you these messages from the past.

URSULA! ARE YOU GETTING THE SIGNAL TOO?! IT'S ART!
BZZ

HE'S CALLING US BACK! *WE'RE GOING HOME!*
WHAT ARE YOU DOING IN THE POOL?
cough
cough
BZZ
BZZ

☐ Ink-based subcutaneous design with a direct link to the auditory canal. Usually employed in extended team situations to facilitate audio-visual communication.

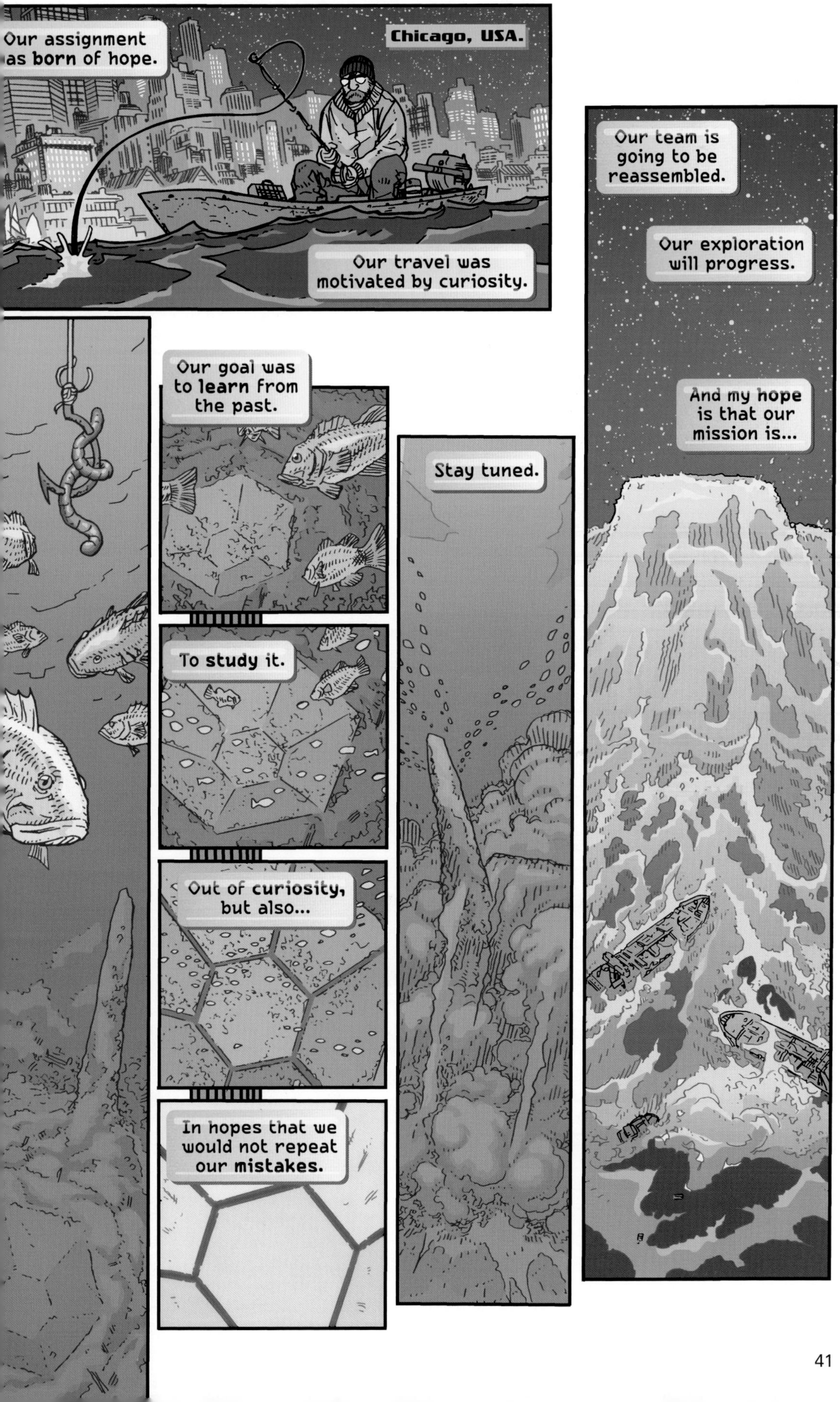

Our goal was to learn from the past.

To study it.

Out of curiosity, but also...

In hopes that we would not repeat our mistakes.

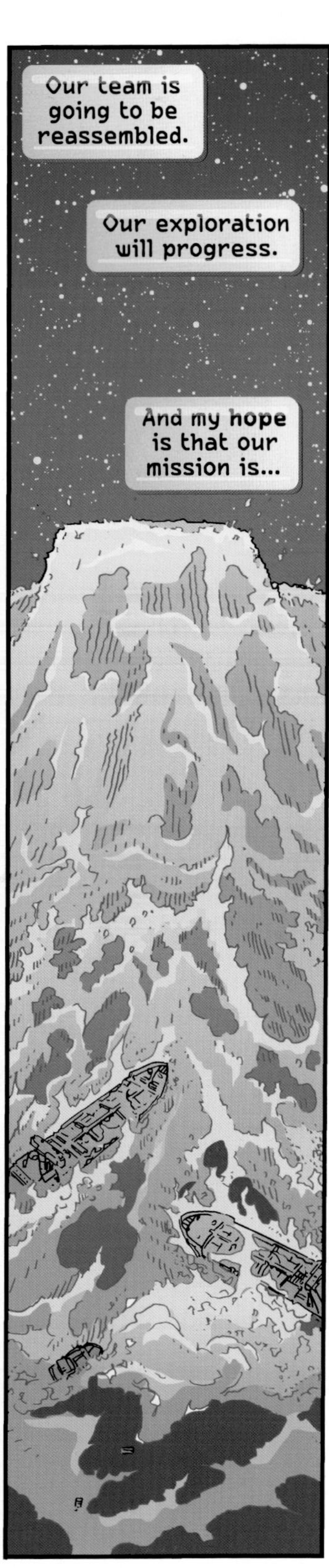

Stay tuned.

Origin and purpose: unknown.

HERBERT TRAVELOGUE

August 2014.

After last week's long rumination and conjecture regarding the absolutely haunting absence of sea apes on the Earth of 2014, I thought it best to detail something of slightly more pedestrian interest. In the name of science, yesterday I took a rather long walk into the wilds of the past and explored a "modern" city street.

While on my journey, lasting a mere thirty minutes, I was verbally accosted by a native in an automobile and my safe-boot was rather rudely exposed to what I initially thought was canine excrement but after lab analysis found to be human. While not seeming like it at the time, this was a stroke of luck, as Philip was able to 5-D scan the fecal sample and extrapolate veritable reams of information from the results.

After proceeding several city blocks, I chanced upon what I can only compare to our modern upload/download centers—but rather than an e-phem connection, the up/downs were achieved with books and what appears to be manual ocular retrieval of information--"reading." We are truly in a different time and place, and today I felt further from home than I ever have before.

When I entered the small "shop," I was given a standard verbal twenty-first-century greeting by a female native and then left to my own devices. It felt like walking into the mythical Library of Congress in the epic poem of Heritec. There was the instant aroma of "pulp" and "ink"--not sim scents but the real thing. It was, I'm not ashamed to admit, intoxicating.

I walked slowly between the long rows of printed novels. So long removed from the heyday of the novel, one forgets how prolific they must have been in the early days. After a while, it became impossible for my eyes to focus, as they jumped from one lurid and alluring simple-hued cover to the next.

Just as I was about to obtain one of these books, uncontrollable nausea took hold of me. My senses were still struggling to acclimate from our travel and my filters were still having trouble screening out the high levels of carcinogens in the ancient atmosphere. As a result, I regurgitated on the female native, just as I was about to test the viability of our native manufactured currency.

As a result, I was unable to obtain a sample from the shop and my admittedly halting conversation (we are all still adjusting our language to overcome the inaccuracies of our predictive translators) with the female native was cut short, as I was promptly ushered out to the city street once again.

I returned home to scan the fecal sample I procured and to rest. This was the longest I have ventured into the native land on my own to date, and I found it as exhausting as it was informative. I made a promise to myself that I would one day return to the "bookshop," procure a book for our sample archive, and continue the conversation with the native female shop guardian.

PAST AWAYS

HEADQUARTERS

In northern Arizona, the PAST AWAYS have made their home in an abandoned missile silo. The team have since made many modifications to both assist with their survival in the 21st century and aid in their quest to return to their own time.

HOLOGRAPHIC SUBMERGED ENTRANCE TUBE

MODIFIED GOVERNMENT MISSILE SILO

FALSE PROJECTORS FOR STAGE 1 ILLUSION AND BASE CONCEALMENT

EXPERIMENTS IN FOUND TECHNOLOGY SAFE-TESTING FACILITY

EXPERIMENTAL HYGIENE AND ENHANCEMENT CHAMBER

UNCONSTRUCTION CHAMBER

QUADCOPTER LANDING PAD

TROPHY ROOM AND CONTAINMENT CENTER FOR POTENTIALLY SENTIENT ARTIFACTS

SENTIENT STAIRCASE WITH TRILEVEL LETHAL-DEFENSE CAPABILITIES

ULTRAVIOLET FICTITIOUS-CHEMICAL PRINTERS

COLORS BY

MARIE ENGER

PAST AWAYS

MATT KINDT SCOTT KOLINS

BILL CRABTREE

KOLINS 2015

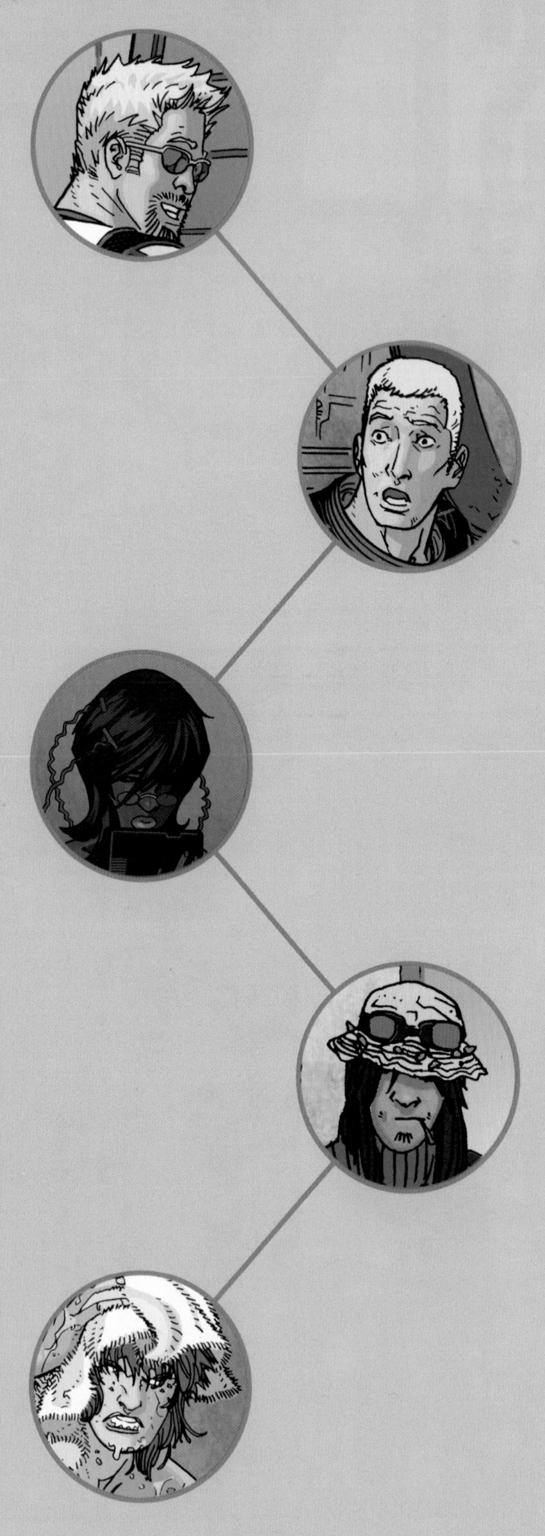

CHECK THIS OUT. I MADE SO MANY IMPROVEMENTS TO OUR HEADQUARTERS. YOU REMEMBER HOW IT ***WAS,*** RIGHT? SO MUCH ***BETTER.***

I'VE BEEN COLLECTING AND STUDYING EVERY ***ARTIFACT*** THAT FALLS OUT OF THE TIME TEAR. I STORE THEM. STUDY THEM. JUST LOOK!

VVVVVVV

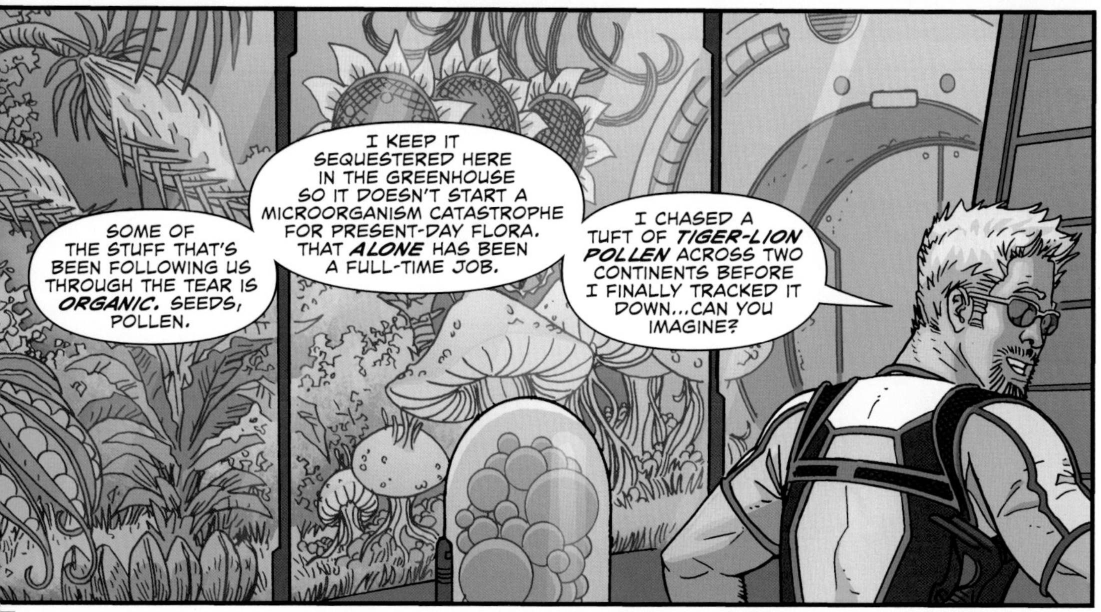

SOME OF THE STUFF THAT'S BEEN FOLLOWING US THROUGH THE TEAR IS ORGANIC. SEEDS, POLLEN.
I KEEP IT SEQUESTERED HERE IN THE GREENHOUSE SO IT DOESN'T START A MICROORGANISM CATASTROPHE FOR PRESENT-DAY FLORA. THAT ALONE HAS BEEN A FULL-TIME JOB.
I CHASED A TUFT OF TIGER-LION POLLEN ACROSS TWO CONTINENTS BEFORE I FINALLY TRACKED IT DOWN...CAN YOU IMAGINE?

❑ Sentient parasite wings which attach to a host, providing flight capabilities but eventually infecting the rontal lobe and causing a new set of wings to grow from the brain stem (killing the host in the process).

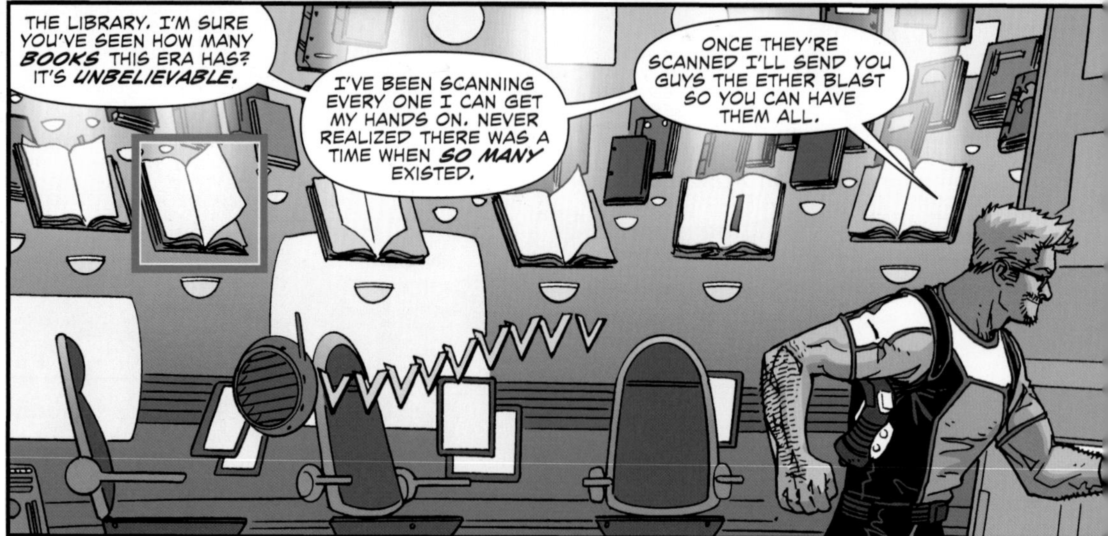

Fiction book entitled *Huckleberry Finn*, by the author Mark Twain, which follows the boyhood adventures of Huck and his escaped slave [? reference needed] companion Jim. While a simple adventure on the surface, the journey down the Mississippi River represents Huck's journey into adulthood and is an indictment of racism. [? reference needed]

THIS IS THE ZOO... FOR ALL OF THE UNFORTUNATE CREATURES THAT END UP FALLING THROUGH THE TIME TEAR.
OBVIOUSLY... DON'T *TOUCH* ANYTHING.

PLENTY OF BUNKS AND SLEEPING QUARTERS.
I CLEANED THE PLACE UP QUITE A BIT. IT WAS...A LITTLE BIT OF A MESS OVER THE LAST YEAR. I LET SOME THINGS GO, I'LL ADMIT.
SPLICE-PARASITE-FREE NOW, THOUGH. SO NO WORRIES.

HIBER- AND ENVIROCHAMBERS ARE ALSO FULLY FUNCTIONAL IF YOU NEED TO REJUVENATE.
SO...? WHAT DO YOU THINK?

WHAT...? IS EVERYTHING OKAY? I THOUGHT THE NEW HEADQUARTERS AND GETTING BACK TOGETHER WOULD BE... ENERGIZING.

OOOKAY, WELL...
EVERYONE, JUST HAVE A SEAT. WE WERE A ***TEAM.*** WE CAN BE THAT AGAIN.
BUT THAT'S ***NOT*** THE ONLY REASON I ASKED YOU ALL TO COME BACK. I'VE REASON TO ***HOPE***--WE ALL DO--THAT WE CAN LEAVE THIS PLACE AND GET BACK TO ***OUR OWN TIME.***

PHIL, YOU OKAY WITH THIS? AFTER ART TRIED TO KILL YOU?
HE ***CAN'T*** KILL ME.
AND YES. I THINK WE DO HAVE A GOOD CHANCE OF RETURNING HOME.
YOU'RE THE LAST ***THING*** I'D LISTEN TO. WHY SHOULD WE GO BACK? WE'RE STUCK HERE FOR A ***REASON.***

PLEASE. ENOUGH WITH YOUR RELIGIOUS PREDESTINATION CRAP. IF ANYTHING, BEING STUCK HERE IS MORE LIKE BEING IN A LAYER OF ***HELL.***

LISTEN...PLEASE. LET'S JUST STICK TOGETHER FOR A ***WEEK.*** WE'LL INVESTIGATE THE TIME TEAR--SEE IF MY THEORY IS RIGHT AND IF IT'S SOMETHING WE CAN EXPLOIT.
IF IT IS, WE CAN GO BACK OR STAY. EVERYONE CAN ***DECIDE*** FOR THEMSELVES.

JUST... TAKE A LITTLE BREAK. ***RELAX.*** I UPDATED THE ROOMS, SO PICK ONE YOU LIKE AND TAKE IT EASY.
WE'LL MEET FOR DINNER AND I'LL RUN YOU ALL THROUGH THE PLANNED COURSE OF ACTION.

Active-cell conference chairs with mini-electrode servos to aid focus and concentration.

URSULA...?
SHOULD WE...YOU WANT TO FIND A ROOM *TOGETHER?*

...HERB...

I DON'T THINK SO. WE'RE A *TEAM* AGAIN. WE NEED TO FALL BACK INTO OUR ROLES.
IF I SHOW *FAVORITISM* TOWARD YOU, IT'S JUST GOING TO CAUSE TENSION IN THE GROUP.

OH. YEAH, YEAH. THAT MAKES SENSE. WELL...I'LL BE DOWN HERE IF YOU WANT TO TALK LATER.

PHIL?

YOU AND ART OKAY NOW? AFTER WHAT HAPPENED...DIDN'T THINK YOU GUYS WOULD BE *TALKIN'* TO EACH OTHER, LET ALONE *WORKIN'* TOGETHER.
GOOD TO SEE YOU GUYS MADE UP.

MARGARET...WE *HAVEN'T* "MADE UP." IF ART COULD BE KILLED...

...I WOULD HAVE KILLED HIM BY NOW.

OH BOY.

☐ Art panel with mood, heart rate, and temperature sensors for live-image feedback. Can be set to either complement or contrast existing mood.

--AND DISCOVERING IT ALL AT THE SAME TIME.
NOT HAVING SECOND THOUGHTS ABOUT THE MISSION, ARE YOU?
NO, ARTHUR. IT'S TOO LATE TO BACK OUT NOW, ANYWAY. IT'S JUST PART OF MY JOB AS PSYCHE OFFICER TO MAKE SURE I KNOW WHERE YOUR HEAD IS AT.
AND DO YOU, URSULA?
OF COURSE I DO. I'M A PROFESSIONAL.
CAN YOU CHANGE THE THEME? YOU KNOW I DON'T LIKE SPACE.
YOU MAY KNOW ME, BUT YOU WILL ALWAYS REMAIN A MYSTERY. IF YOU CAN'T STAND SPACE, THEN WHY DID YOU JOIN THE CORPS?
FOR THE PEOPLE.
ANYWAY, WE'RE NOT GOING INTO SPACE. IN THEORY, WE'RE NOT GOING TO BE MOVING AT ALL.

Standard item-conveyance device with finite interior storage. Lacks any hover, teleportation, or weight-transference capabilities.
Before.
BADUM
BADUM
BADUM

GARRRRGGG!

Before.
IT'S GOOD TO SEE YOU. I'VE MISSED YOU SO MUCH.
I WAS THINKING ABOUT YOU YESTERDAY. THE APARTMENT WAS QUIET, AND I WAS REMEMBERING YOU SINGING IN THE WASHROOM WHEN YOU WOULD TAKE YOUR BATHS.
I LOVED THAT SOUND. LIKE YOU DIDN'T HAVE A CARE IN THE WORLD. JUST THIS AIMLESS SINGING. NO SONG IN PARTICULAR. IT WOULD MAKE ME LAUGH WHEN YOU--
YOU COULD HEAR THAT? THAT'S SO EMBARRASSING!

The modern cemetery is capable of scanning a living human and solid-gram printing them into space for a full-scale living interaction, complete th tactile and audio feedback. Brain scans and personality models make it possible to interact with loved ones long after they have passed away.

Before.
DROP THE COOLING CORE NOW, OR WE'LL ALL BE *KILLED,* YOU *SPINELESS--*
CALCULATING COST OF REPLACEMENT AGAINST USE OF COOLING CORE...PLEASE WAIT MOMENTARILY.

Rescue and retrieval drone. Primarily used to keep morale high during high-
k gas-giant-mining operations.

AOOGA AOOGA AOOGA
AOOGA AOOGA AOOGA
AOOGA
AOOGA
AOOGA
AOOGA
WHO SET THE ALARM? AND WHY IS IT SO *LOUD?*
YOU SLEEP WELL?
...
YOU'RE STILL NOT SLEEPING? YOU SHOULD, PHIL. IT'S NOT HEALTHY--
FORGET IT.

I APOLOGIZE FOR THE RUDE AWAKENING, BUT SOMETHING HAS HAPPENED THAT REQUIRES OUR IMMEDIATE INTERVENTION. SOMETHING VERY... *UH*... ***BIG*** HAS EMERGED THROUGH THE TIME TEAR. IT'S FORTUITOUS THAT WE'VE ALL FINALLY GOTTEN BACK TOGETHER.
EVERYONE IN YOUR ACTION SUITS. WE'LL RECONVENE AT THE LAUNCH PAD IN FIVE. I'LL ***EXPLAIN*** ON THE WAY.
TRUST ME, GUYS.
Five minutes later.
EVER SINCE WE ARRIVED, I KNOW WE'VE BECOME... BASICALLY ***IMMORTAL.*** DUE TO THE TIMESTREAM PHYSICS, WE CAN'T DIE ***BEFORE*** WE WERE BORN. WE CAN'T KILL OUR GREAT-GREAT-GRANDFATHERS.
TIME PROTECTS ITSELF. CONUNDRUMS CAN'T HAPPEN. AND WE'VE EACH ***PROVEN*** THIS NEARLY EVERY DAY SINCE WE ARRIVED.
WE ***KNOW*** THIS. SO WHAT'S THE POINT? WE'VE BEEN LIVING HERE FOR A YEAR. NOTHING NEW HAS HAPPENED. ***NOTHING'S*** CHANGED.
BUT IT ***HAS!*** I'LL EXPLAIN EVERYTHING...

Four hours later.
Chicago.
...SO THAT'S THE SCIENCE OF IT ALL. LONG STORY SHORT--I AM NOW ABLE TO PREDICT THE TIME-TEAR ERUPTIONS. THAT'S WHAT'S HAPPENING IN CHICAGO. RIGHT NOW.

MY HOPE IS THAT WE STUDY WHATEVER COMES OUT OF THE TEAR AND MAYBE...JUST ***MAYBE...*** WE CAN SNEAK BACK THROUGH THE TEAR. BACK TO OUR ***OWN TIME.***
WE'VE HEARD YOUR THEORIES AND PROMISES ***COUNTLESS TIMES*** BEFORE, ARTHUR. WE'RE STUCK HERE. THERE'S NO GETTING BACK. WHAT MAKES THIS ANY...

...DIFFERENT?
...MOTHER OF GODS...!

WATCH OUT!
IT'S SWINGING TOWARD US!

Unknown technology. Manufacture date postdates current database.

I'M--
I'M SURE ART WILL *GET OUT* IN TIME...
PHIL?! WHAT--
KSHHH
Herbert Travel Journal:
We went back to this time to document the distant past.
We went back to explore a culture long gone.
HMMMMMMM
Unknown technology. Manufacture date postdates current database.

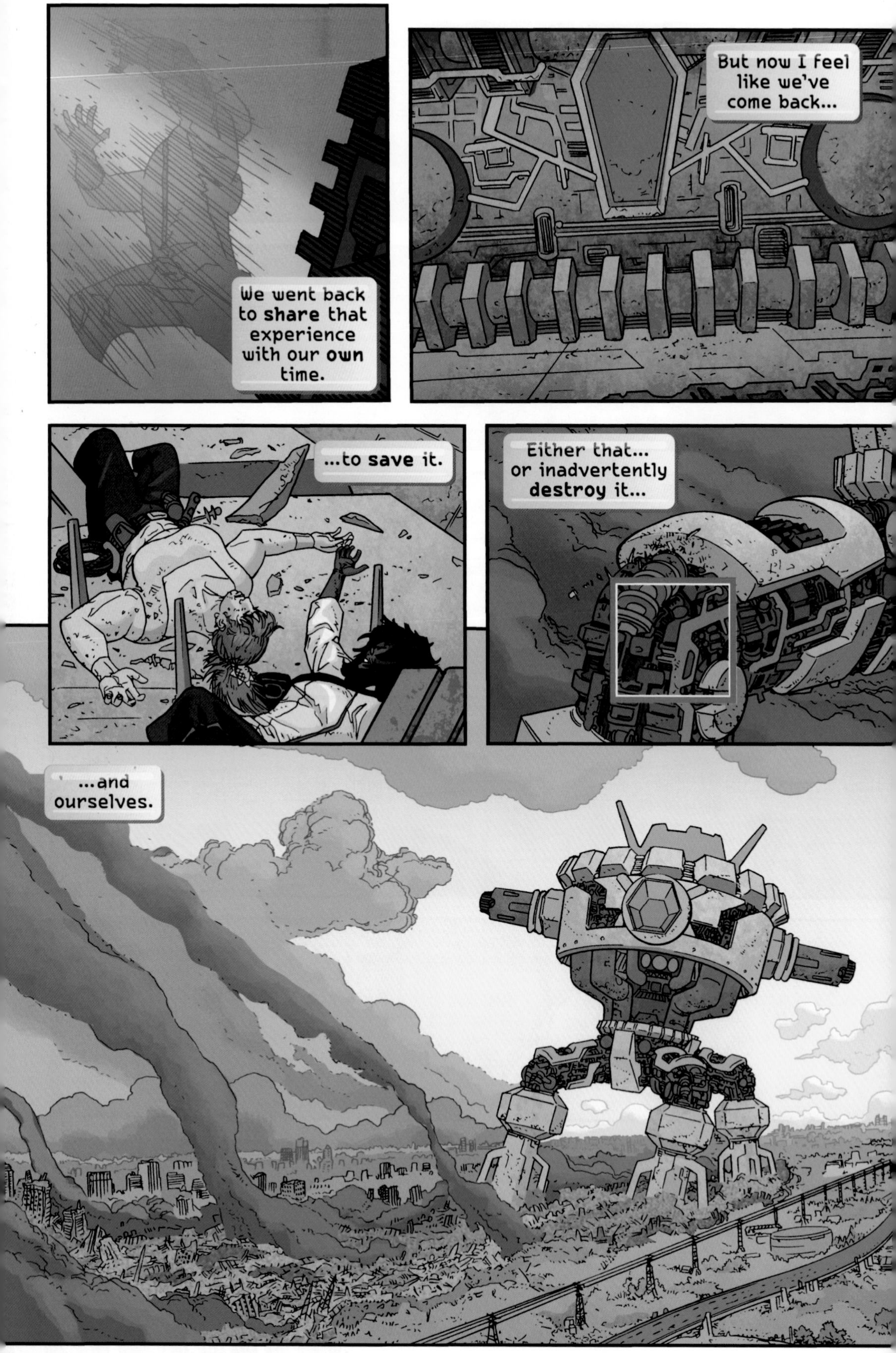

We went back to share that experience with our own time.

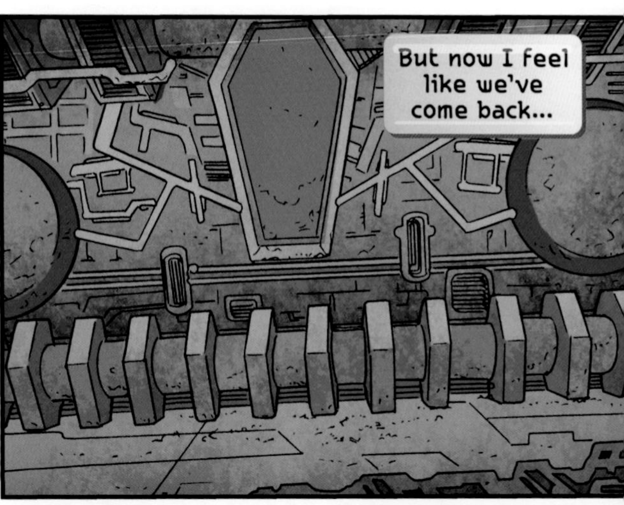

But now I feel like we've come back...

...to save it.

Either that... or inadvertently destroy it...

...and ourselves.

Unknown technology. Manufacture date postdates current database.

HERBERT TRAVELOGUE

September 2014.

Arthur has yet to manufacture a nutrition dispenser, so today, once again, I took to the streets of the twenty-first century to find victuals. Food preparation, you will be surprised to learn, is prevalent in this era and not confined to historical reenactments and boutique cafeterias. One may find an establishment serving custom comestibles on every street corner.

My resolve steeled by hunger, I vowed to forget my last food expedition in the city and strike out with renewed optimism. On entering the heavily branded feeding establishment I was immediately struck by the flood of choices presented to me. But upon closer study I realized that these choices were simply variations on five simple ingredients. Realizing this, I simply ordered the "#1." Long minutes later, my meal finally arrived, and I found a seat in the common area to further study and actually partake in the unique custom of eating in this primitive era.

My chemical and bioanalysis of the "food" given to me was endlessly fascinating. One forgets, in our modern world, how streamlined and efficient humanity has become. We, in modern times, are used to simply taking one daily supplement in the morning that fulfills all the body's dietary and nutritional requirements, leaving the individual free to pursue intellectual pursuits without the hindrance of periodic pauses for sustenance.

However, in the more crude times that I find myself lost in, nutritional sustenance is crudely and inefficiently prepared, causes great harm to the environment, and creates tremendous waste byproducts. The incessant hunger that I face is a constant irritant, causing me many delays in my studies and a marked reduction in productivity.

The resolution of my foray into this century's food is something better left to the imagination. I'll skip the rest of the grisly details; suffice it to say that the entire ingesting experience was absolutely horrifying. What happened later, back at headquarters, was equally, if not more, horrifying, as the fried product of a bygone era fought its way through my system and forcefully ejected itself without my consent.

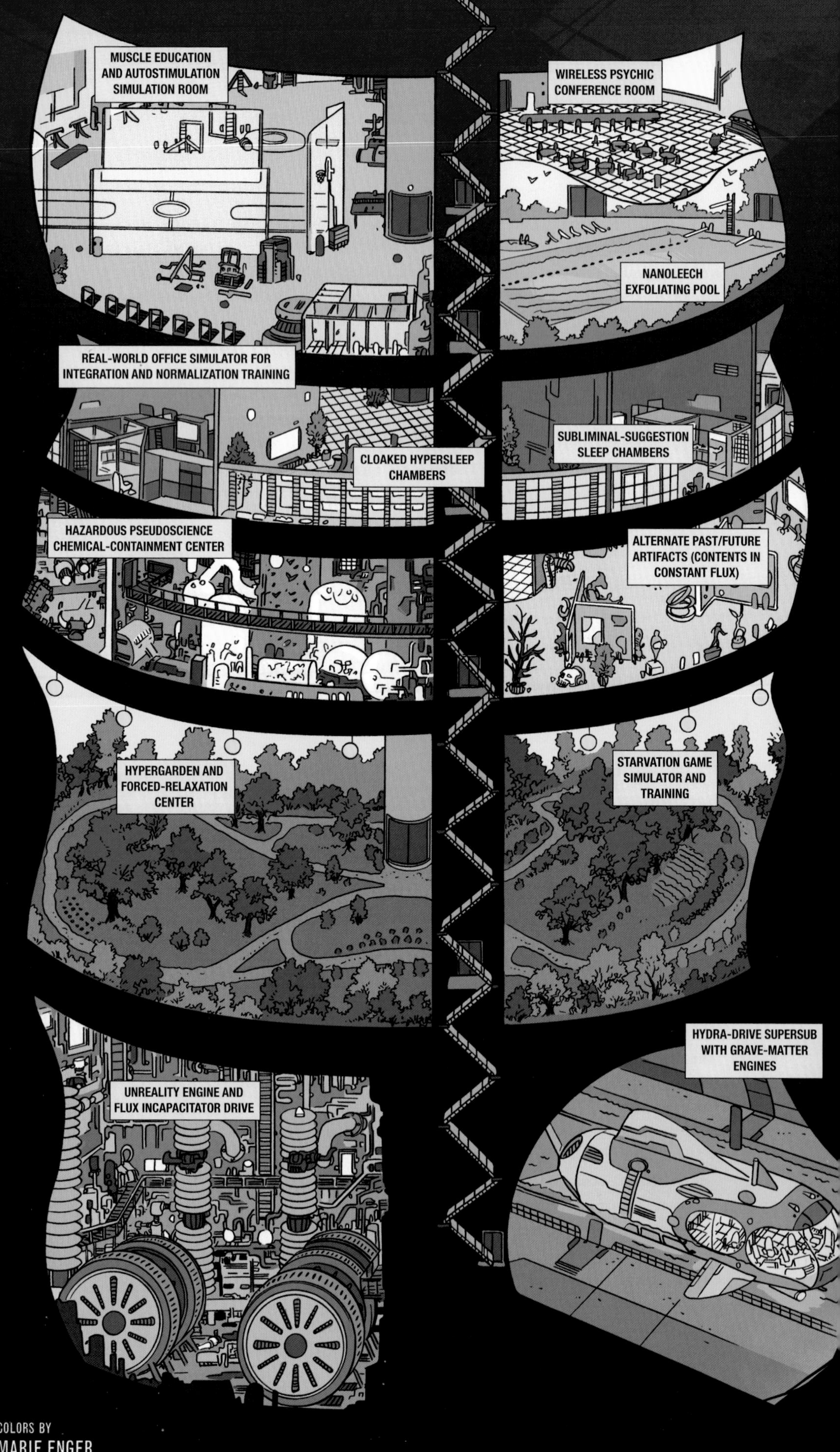
MUSCLE EDUCATION AND AUTOSTIMULATION SIMULATION ROOM
WIRELESS PSYCHIC CONFERENCE ROOM
NANOLEECH EXFOLIATING POOL
REAL-WORLD OFFICE SIMULATOR FOR INTEGRATION AND NORMALIZATION TRAINING
CLOAKED HYPERSLEEP CHAMBERS
SUBLIMINAL-SUGGESTION SLEEP CHAMBERS
HAZARDOUS PSEUDOSCIENCE CHEMICAL-CONTAINMENT CENTER
ALTERNATE PAST/FUTURE ARTIFACTS (CONTENTS IN CONSTANT FLUX)
HYPERGARDEN AND FORCED-RELAXATION CENTER
STARVATION GAME SIMULATOR AND TRAINING
HYDRA-DRIVE SUPERSUB WITH GRAVE-MATTER ENGINES
UNREALITY ENGINE AND FLUX INCAPACITATOR DRIVE

COLORS BY
MARIE ENGER

PAST
AWAYS
MATT KINDT SCOTT KOLINS
BILL CRABTREE
KOLINS '16

11:50AM
April 22
Q NEWZ
...IMAGES ARE BEYOND BELIEF. BUT, REMARKABLY, THE DEATH TOLL SO FAR IS LOW.
EXCLUSIVE
CHICAGO IN TURMOIL AS HUNDREDS OF MILES OF DESTRUCTION LIE SMO

11:54AM
April 22
Q NEWZ
THE "ROBOT," FOR LACK OF A BETTER TERM, HAS MOVED SLOWLY ENOUGH FOR RESIDENTS IN ITS PATH TO EVACUATE SAFELY.
EXCLUSIVE
STATE OF EMERGENCY ISSUED FOR ENTIRE STATE OF ILLINOIS

Zoom X 10
WE HAVE AN EXPERT PANEL HERE TO DISCUSS THE THEORIES BEHIND THIS STRANGE DISASTER. IS IT A TERRORIST ATTACK? INTELLIGENT LIFE FROM ANOTHER PLANET? OR THE END TIMES? WE'LL DISCUSS ALL OF THAT AND MORE, AFTER THE BREAK...
PRESIDENT ORDERS AIR FORCE TO INTERCEPT "ROBOT"

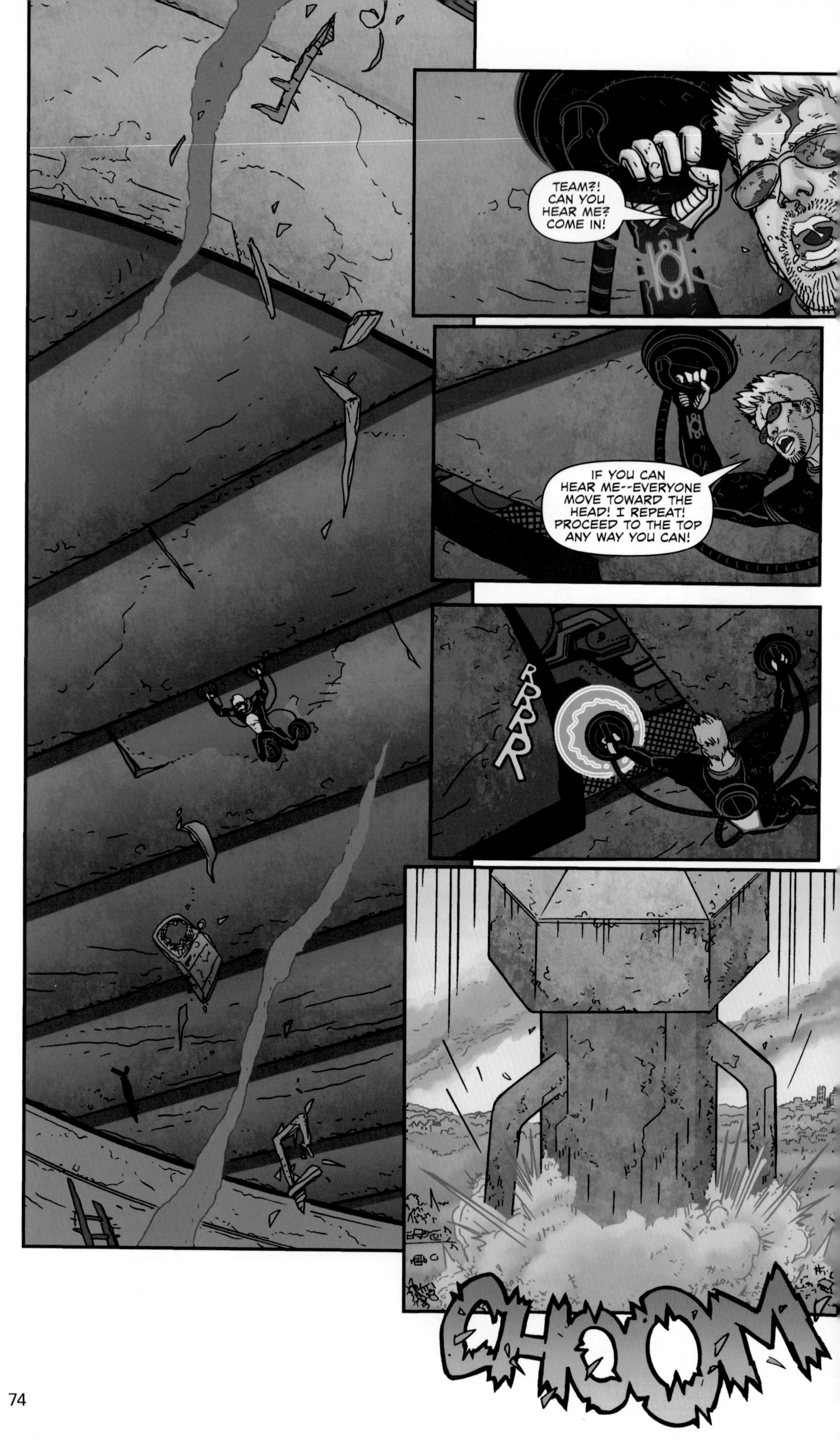
TEAM?! CAN YOU HEAR ME? COME IN!
IF YOU CAN HEAR ME--EVERYONE MOVE TOWARD THE HEAD! I REPEAT! PROCEED TO THE TOP ANY WAY YOU CAN!
RRRR
CHOOM

Shock suit designed for full flexibility and fitted with microsecond adaptability to lessen traumatic impact.

WELL... WE MADE IT.

MUST BE SCRAMBLING OUR COMMUNICATIONS, OR ART WOULD HAVE BEEN SHOUTING OUT ORDERS BY NOW.
DO YOU THINK THE REST OF THEM ARE OKAY?
IT'S UP TO US TO FIGURE OUT HOW TO STOP THIS THING.

BEST BET IN MY EXPERIENCE IS TO HIT 'EM LOW. GO FOR THE LEGS. IMMOBILIZE IT FIRST.

ARE YOU SURE? SHOULDN'T WE TRY TO CONTACT THE OTHERS?

MARGARET... I'M NOT SURE. MAYBE WE SHOULD WAIT UNTIL WE HEA FROM ART...?

AHHHG!

I'M NOT SURE...*nghh*... SO GROSS...

I THINK I'M GONNA BE SICK... THE SMELL...IT'S GETTING TO ME, MARGARET...
THE FUMES... IT'S EXUDING SOME KIND OF DEFENSIVE MIST...
WE GOTTA HURRY, OR WE'RE GONNA LOSE MORE THAN THE FIGHT...

WE JUST NEED TO KILL THIS THING.
PSSSS

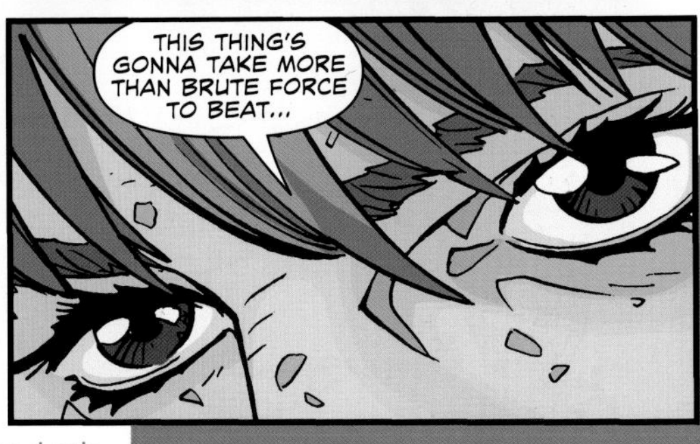

THIS THING'S GONNA TAKE MORE THAN BRUTE FORCE TO BEAT...

] Canvas high-tops: canvas uppers resting on a quality vulcanized rubber sole with manual-tie laces. Lacking adaptive traction sense.

Before.
"BECOMING ONE OF THE KNIGHT'S ORDER REQUIRES TWO THINGS, MARGARET. ONE: PROVE YOUR STRENGTH.
"TWO: PROVE YOUR CUNNING.
"STRENGTH AND VIOLENCE WILL NOT HELP YOU SURVIVE ON THE SMALL MOON OF FELIX LX-719. THE MOON IS DESOLATE. NO FOOD OR WATER. YOU WILL BE STRANDED THERE FOR SIXTY DAYS.
"HOWEVER, YOU WILL NOT BE ALONE. WE HAVE STRANDED A VICIOUS, FERAL MODIFIED CAMELJACK ON THE MOON, AS WELL. YOUR TEST IS SIMPLY TO SURVIVE FOR THE FULL SIXTY DAYS."
"WE KNOW IT SEEMED HOPELESS WHEN YOU FIRST GOT THERE.

The cameljack is a technohybrid animal created by the Evolutioneers. A useful crossbreed of camel, cow, kangaroo, and rhinoceros. Its usefulness is offset by its utterly vicious nature.

"THAT WAS THE POINT. NO FOOD. NO WATER.
"JUST THE CREATURE.
"IF YOU KILLED IT, YOU WOULD ONLY HAVE LIVED FOR ANOTHER WEEK. BUT, AS YOU REALIZED, ITS MEAT WOULD GO BAD AND IT WOULD STOP MAKING POTABLE FLUIDS.
"IF YOU'D KILLED IT THE FIRST DAY...
"...YOU WOULD HAVE BEEN DEAD BY DAY TEN."
YOUR CONTINUED EXISTENCE IS YOUR PASSING GRADE, MARGARET. CONGRATULATIONS.

Now.
PLACE IS FULL OF AUTOMATED DEFENSIVE MECHANISMS. LIKE A LIVING ORGANISM. IT'S LITERALLY PRODUCING ANTIBODIES...

ANY IDEAS?

PLENTY.

CARE TO SHARE? IT'S GETTING A LITTLE CROWDED IN HERE.
TENSILE STRENGTH MIGHT BE JUST ENOUGH. WE'LL HAVE TO BE QUICK.

WHAT THE--?!

FOLLOW ME.
THE ACID SHOULD BURN A HOLE BIG ENOUGH FOR US TO GET THROUGH.
BUT YOU MIGHT WANT TO HOLD YOUR BREATH.
THE ACID PUSTULES ARE EXUDING A DEADLY HALLUCINOGEN.
OH... OHHHHHH...
NOW YOU TELL ME...
Hallucinogen/acid hybrid defense mechanism that serves a small part of a larger evolutionary autoimmune defense, which mutated over hundreds of years inside a closed artificial environment. Curiously, designed not to kill but to incapacitate and expel toxic agents.

THANK YOU, PHIL...FOR NOT... FOR NOT LEAVING ME BEHIND...

WHY WOULD I LEAVE YOU BEHIND...?

IF WE GET BACK, IT WON'T BE AT THE COST OF MY LIFE. I'VE SPENT MY ENTIRE EXISTENCE FIGHTING PEOPLE LIKE YOU, ARTHUR. WE BOTH KNOW I'VE BEEN PROGRAMMED SO THAT I CAN'T KILL ANOTHER HUMAN BEING.
BUT THAT WON'T KEEP ME--
--FROM MAKING THE REST OF YOUR LIFE MISERABLE.

Now.
THIS THING IS SCRAMBLING OUR COMMUNICATIONS. BUT I'M HOPING OUR EXTENSIVE TRAINING AND PROFESSIONAL INSTINCTS END UP SENDING YOU ALL IN THE RIGHT DIRECTION.

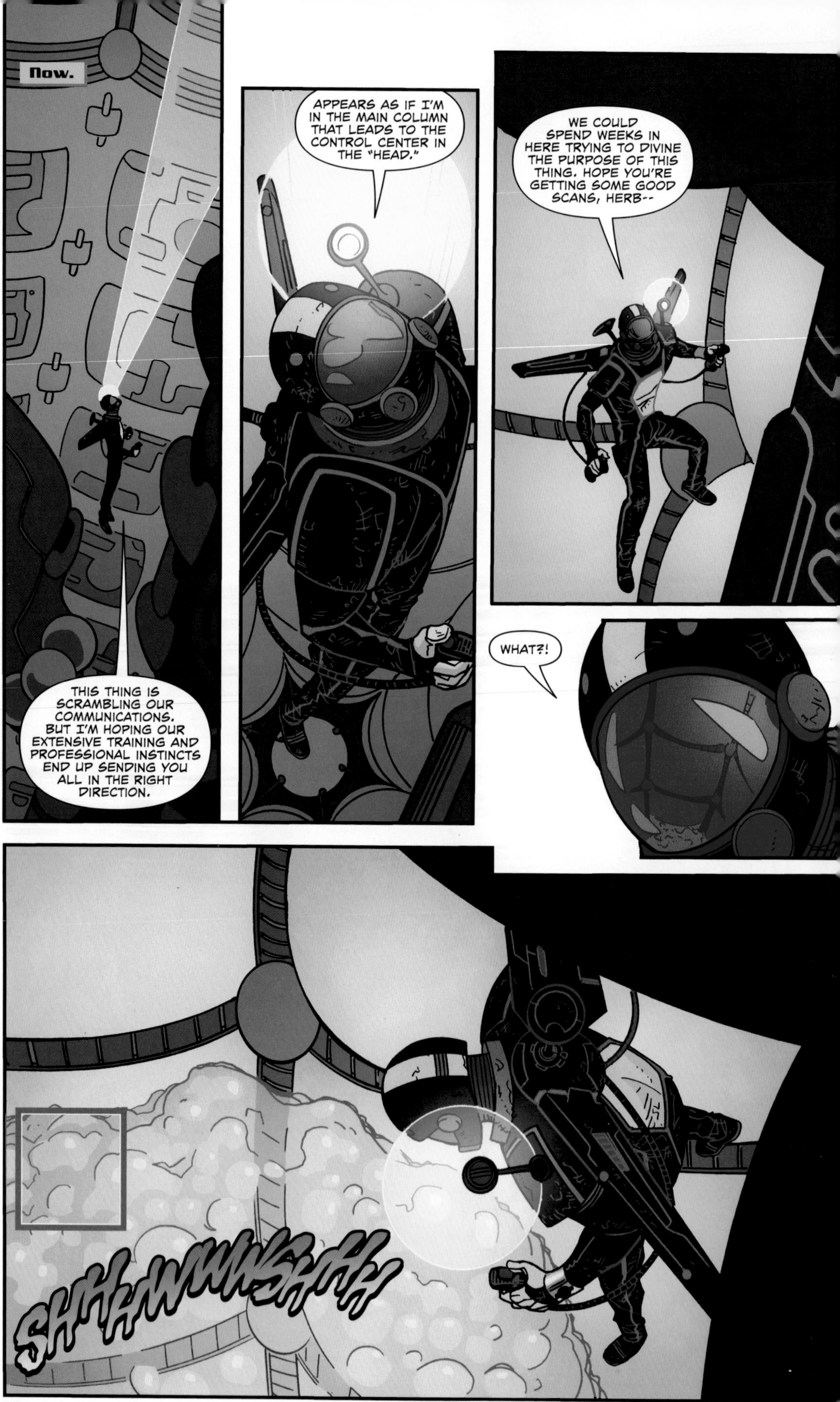

APPEARS AS IF I'M IN THE MAIN COLUMN THAT LEADS TO THE CONTROL CENTER IN THE "HEAD."

WE COULD SPEND WEEKS IN HERE TRYING TO DIVINE THE PURPOSE OF THIS THING. HOPE YOU'RE GETTING SOME GOOD SCANS, HERB--

WHAT?!

Artificially enhanced spinal fluid with basic sentience and programmed nonlethal defensive capabilities.

THE DEFENSIVE MECHANISMS IN THIS THING SEEM LIKE CONTEMPORARY TECHNOLOGY.

CONTEMPORARY TO *OUR* TIME.

NEARLY THERE... FEW MORE STEPS...

I JUST HOPE...

Before.
YOU ALL MADE IT!
YOU ARE THE TOP OF THE LINE. THE ELITE IN ALL OF YOUR FIELDS. AND I'M PROUD TO BE YOUR LEADER.
JUST AS YOU ARE ELITE, I TOO HAVE UNDERGONE RIGOROUS TRAINING AND TESTS. SO YOU CAN REST ASSURED THAT I AM BEST AT WHAT I DO. AND WHAT I DO IS...
LEAD!
YOU ARE PUTTING YOUR LIVES IN MY HANDS. AND BELIEVE ME WHEN I TELL YOU--
--I AM UP TO BEARING THE WEIGHT OF THAT RESPONSIBILITY. AND IN TIME, YOU WILL EACH COME TO SEE ME AS...

☐ Mission control proving ground designed to humiliate unqualified recruits.

WHAT IS THIS THING?

☐ Spectrometer capable of recording and scanning on every known light and sound wavelength in existence. Also capable of timestreaming music from every era of recorded history.

IT IS...
Herbert Travel Journal:
It was amazing.
HERB. STRIP THE PROGRAMMING FROM THIS THING'S NAV BANKS. HOPEFULLY IT CREATES A CONUNDRUM. IF HE CAN'T FIND HIS WAY BACK HERE, HE CAN'T EVER ARRIVE.

I did what Art told me to. I didn't share all of my findings with the team. I felt a little bad about that. But with the poisoned history that Arthur and Phil have, I thought it best.

The torso was from a model similar to Phil. Complete artificial intelligence. It could feel the entire range of emotions and feelings that a normal human could.

I downloaded its travel nav files with a simple ether-hack--along with everything else.
It turns out the AI torso had once been complete, like Phil. But mission control from our era had **streamlined** and **beefed** it up. Taking out all unnecessary interactive interfaces (face and hands). It was the only organism robust enough to run the giant simulacrum...the "robot" that we were inside.
THERE'S OUR WAY OUT! THE FLOOR--!

He/it was a proof of concept. It had been jumping through time ever since. Stopping for several days to refuel--tapping Earth's energy as it walked--recharging for its next jump through time.

The time tear's temporal gravity had trapped it in an endless cycle. Mission control hadn't devised a way for it to break out of a jump cycle and return. It had been jumping for decades. Often ending up outside the atmosphere or under the ocean and unnoticed. Time was protecting itself from conundrums. Therefore, it couldn't die.

I couldn't help it. All I could do was pull out a critical piece of its chronomotor. And hope that the conundrum of me holding its energy source when it disappeared...would mean that it would never return.

His/its consciousness was trapped in a prison it couldn't escape. And in a body that couldn't die. I tell myself that the consciousness inside is simply artificial. It can't feel. It's not torture.

Later, when I went back and looked at the scans, I detected a high-frequency signal on a loop that the AI had been broadcasting. Just two words:

NEW TARGETS ACQUIRED. PERMISSION TO ENGAGE.
GRANTED.
"Help me."

I hope we did.
But I guess only time will tell.
Meanwhile, we've got our own problems...
HEADS UP, TEAM! INCOMING!

☐ Antiquated "jet" fighters for use in conventional air warfare. Piloted by humans and lacking any empathy safeties on explosive payloads.

We, like it,
were out of time.
Unkillable.
And utterly
lost.
I'LL BE
DAMNED. EVERY
ONE OF THEM
WAS A DUD.

HERBERT TRAVELOGUE

October 2014.

The limits of this bygone era's mass-media distribution are many. One cannot simply *ether-read* or *subconscious-see* the latest *scribe* or *viztory*. One has to consciously make an effort not only to seek out the latest entertainment but also determine how one will ingest said entertainment.

For today's foray into the twenty-first century, I decided to absorb a *film* at the *cinema*. I purchased a paper (!) ticket and was ushered into the multiplex. Once inside, the true limitations of in-person viewing became apparent. With only twenty screens to display the crude visual stories, one can only wonder how many unique and creative voices are silenced simply by the lack of venue.

As a true explorer of this strange time and place, I am committed to subjecting myself to every aspect of the local experience. Once again, I noticed that the viewing of entertainment and the imbibing of un-nutrition are linked. I chose a small paper (!) bag of popped corn (with a mildly toxic coating of a grease-like butter simulation) and a box of caramels encased within a thin layer of a synthetic (inedible) simulated chocolate. I guessed at the time that nearly every ingredient in this *candy* was simulated and later scans and analysis would prove me right.

The film itself began. A simple reflected-light arrangement was projected onto a screen. To say that the film-delivery system was crude would be an understatement. There were no subcutaneous ganglia feeds to simulate emotions. There were no hallucinogenic fumes to aid viewing in four dimensions. As I said, crude. But . . . once I was able to (mostly) get over these seemingly insurmountable shortcomings, I was treated to a rather intriguing story.

Yes. You have read that correctly. I was treated to a narrative in a full three acts. It certainly contained *stars* as we know them—but unlike the drivel we have grown accustomed to in our era, they were attempting *acting*. As obvious at it was in its presentation, this film actually had a message. Or, if it didn't have a message, it seemed to be simulating one. The entire affair stands in stark contrast to the six-to-ten-minute mind bursts we have grown accustomed to being entertained by. And rather than a six-minute collage of artificial explosions and sexual liaisons, the films of this era were still attempting to couch these same elements in the framework of a narrative. A fascinating (if somewhat tedious) experience.

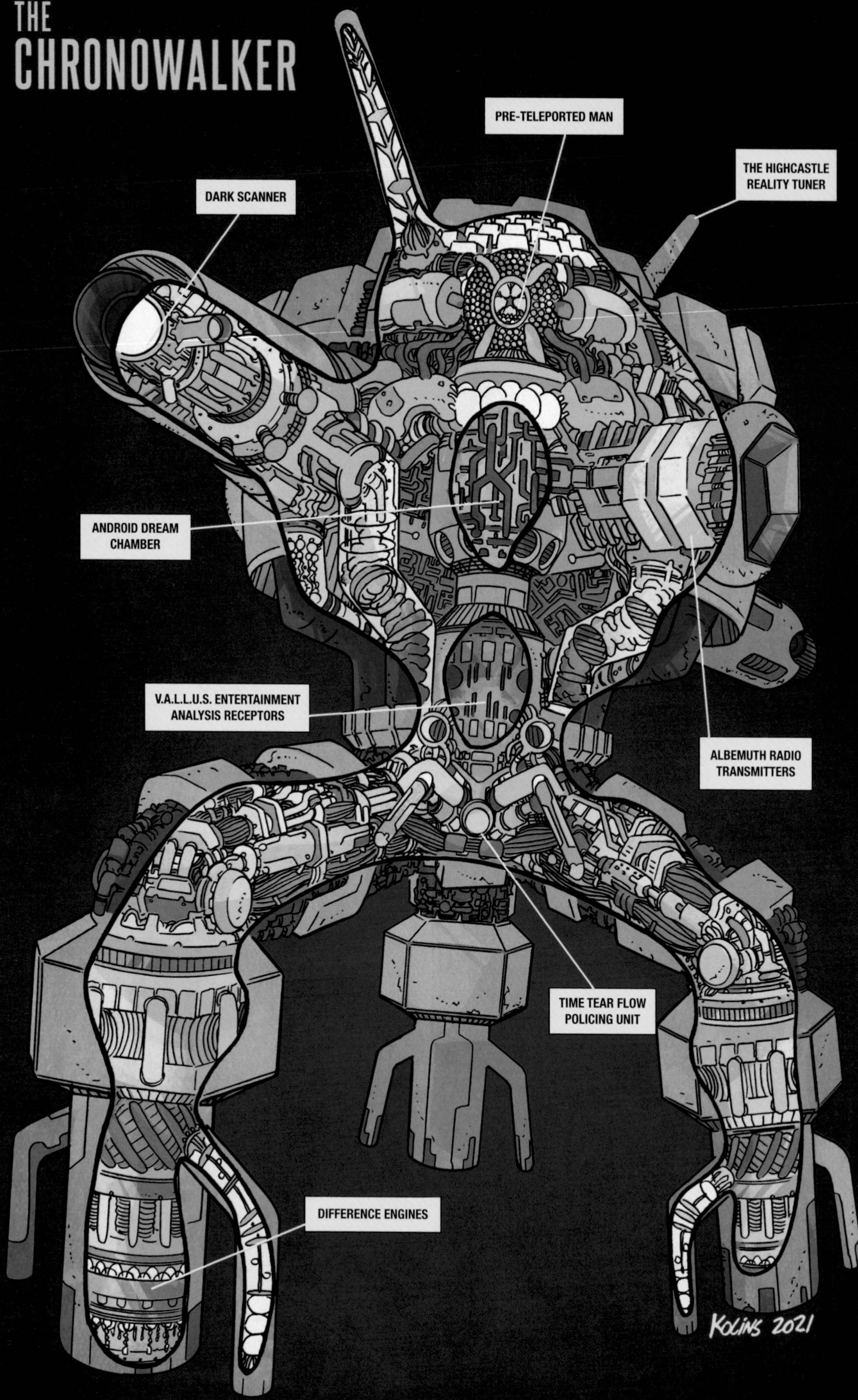
THE
CHRONOWALKER
PRE-TELEPORTED MAN
THE HIGHCASTLE REALITY TUNER
DARK SCANNER
ANDROID DREAM CHAMBER
V.A.L.L.U.S. ENTERTAINMENT ANALYSIS RECEPTORS
ALBEMUTH RADIO TRANSMITTERS
TIME TEAR FLOW POLICING UNIT
DIFFERENCE ENGINES
KOLINS 2021

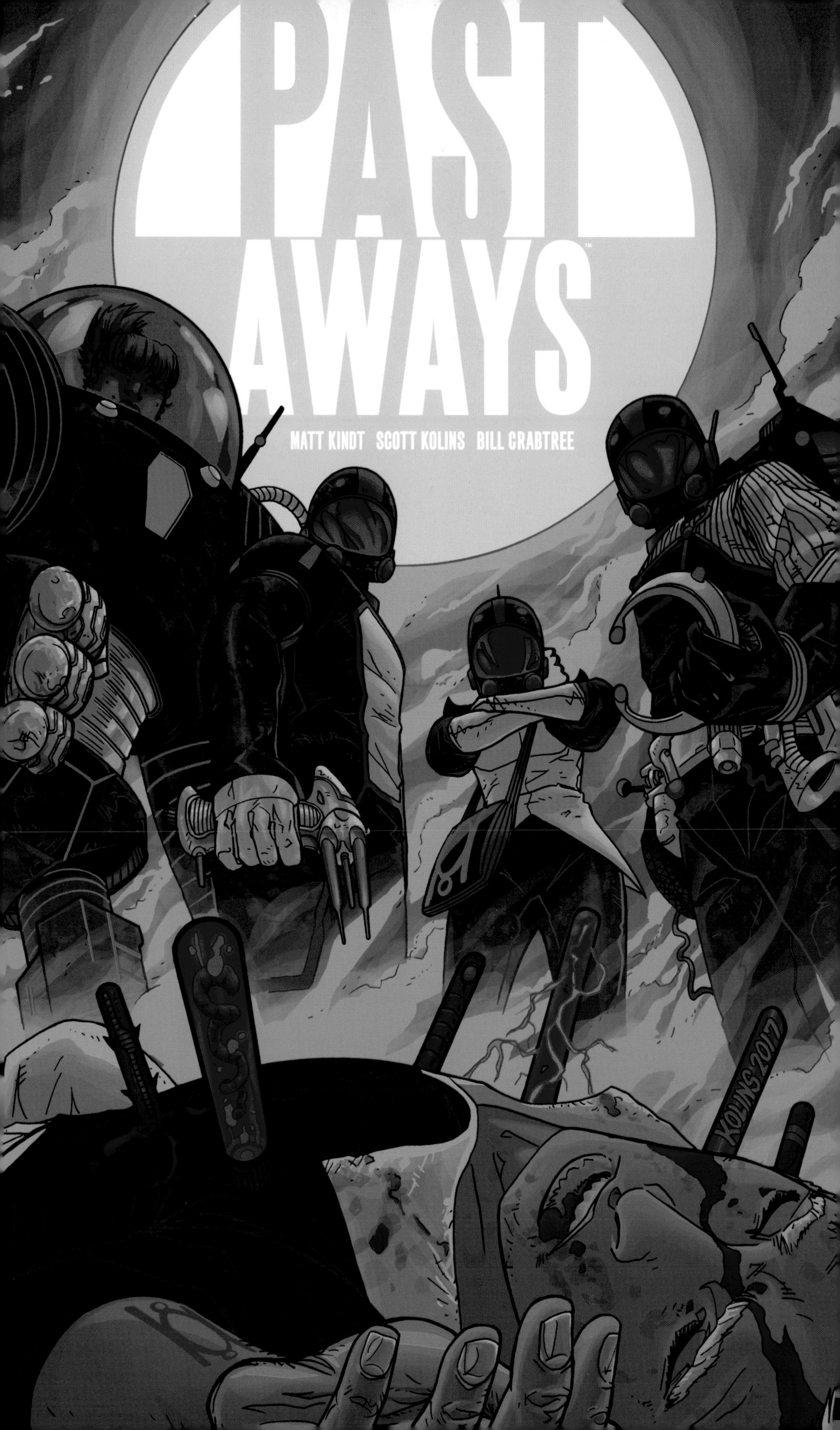
PAST AWAYS™
MATT KINDT SCOTT KOLINS BILL CRABTREE
KOLINS 2017

"YOU'RE NOT GOING TO BELIEVE ANY OF IT. I PROMISE YOU."
"TRY ME, ARTHUR."
WE'RE A TEAM OF EXPLORERS SENT FROM A MILLION YEARS IN THE FUTURE TO YOUR PRESENT. WE WERE SUPPOSED TO SPEND TWENTY-FOUR HOURS IN YOUR TIME, EXPLORE, RECORD, AND REPORT ON THE NATURE OF THIS ERA, THEN RETURN HOME.
THAT WAS OVER A YEAR AGO.
I CAN TELL YOU THINK I'M CRAZY.
NO...PLEASE. CONTINUE. I'M HERE TO LISTEN, NOT JUDGE.
WE'RE STRANDED HERE. NOT ONLY THAT, WHEN WE CAME THROUGH TO THE TWENTY-FIRST CENTURY, WE CREATED A TIME TEAR.
A HOLE IN REALITY THAT'S IN CONSTANT FLUX AND SEEMS TO BE DUMPING...STRANGE, uh... THINGS FROM OTHER ERAS INTO THIS TIMELINE.
...
YEAH. SEE. I HAD A FEELING I SHOULD HAVE MAYBE SUGAR-COATED SOME OF THIS.
NO, PLEASE. CONTINUE.
WHERE TO BEGIN...
LET'S KEEP IT SIMPLE. WHY DON'T WE START WITH YESTERDAY?
WELL... YESTERDAY. LET ME TELL YOU ABOUT YESTERDAY...WE WERE ALL...

Collected analog texts in an outmoded format and rife with incorrect information on the machinations of the mind.

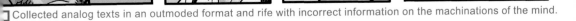

"...SOMEWHERE IN THE PACIFIC."

WE'VE GOT TO GET TO THE *NERVE CENTER* OF THIS THING!

URSULA? YOU GETTING ANY *SYMPATHETIC PSYCHIC RESIDUE?* IS IT *SENTIENT?* CAN WE *HELP* IT?

IT'S...THERE'S *DEFINITELY* INTELLIGENCE HERE...BUT IT'S CONFUSED...IN SOME KIND OF *FEEDBACK LOOP*...IT'S TALKING TO ITSELF...
IT'S THINKING THE SAME THOUGHT OVER AND OVER AGAIN...

"...BRING THEM BACK, MUST BRING THEM BACK..."

WHATEVER'S CONTROLLING THIS THING...IT'S HAVING SOME *EMOTIONAL ISSUES...*
ART?!

MARGE!
MARGE!
WE DON'T KNOW WHAT
WE'RE DEALING WITH
YET--DON'T--
BLRRTCH

☐ Fleshy ersatz skin designed to withstand temporal shifts and extreme temperature fluctuation, but susceptible to blunt force trauma.

I'M HEADED TO THE CONTROL CENTER...
"I HAVE TO BE HONEST. AS A TEAM, WE NEVER REALLY GELLED LIKE I'D HOPED."
KEEP IT OCCUPIED...
"WE SEEM TO ALWAYS GET THE JOB DONE, BUT COORDINATING THE TEAM HAS BEEN PROBLEMATIC."
NEARLY THERE...
"A MONTH EARLIER, SOMETHING HAD COME THROUGH THE TIME TEAR AND DESTROYED A SWATH OF CHICAGO. I'M SURE YOU SAW IT ON THE NEWS.
"WE WERE LUCKY THIS TIME. THE ANOMALY APPEARED OVER THE PACIFIC. THERE WERE NO CASUALTIES.

"BUT DEFEATING THIS THING WAS ANOTHER STORY."
Ursula: Psych officer
Herb: Documentaria
Marge: Weapons Specialist

Phil: Technology Specialist
Art: Team Leader

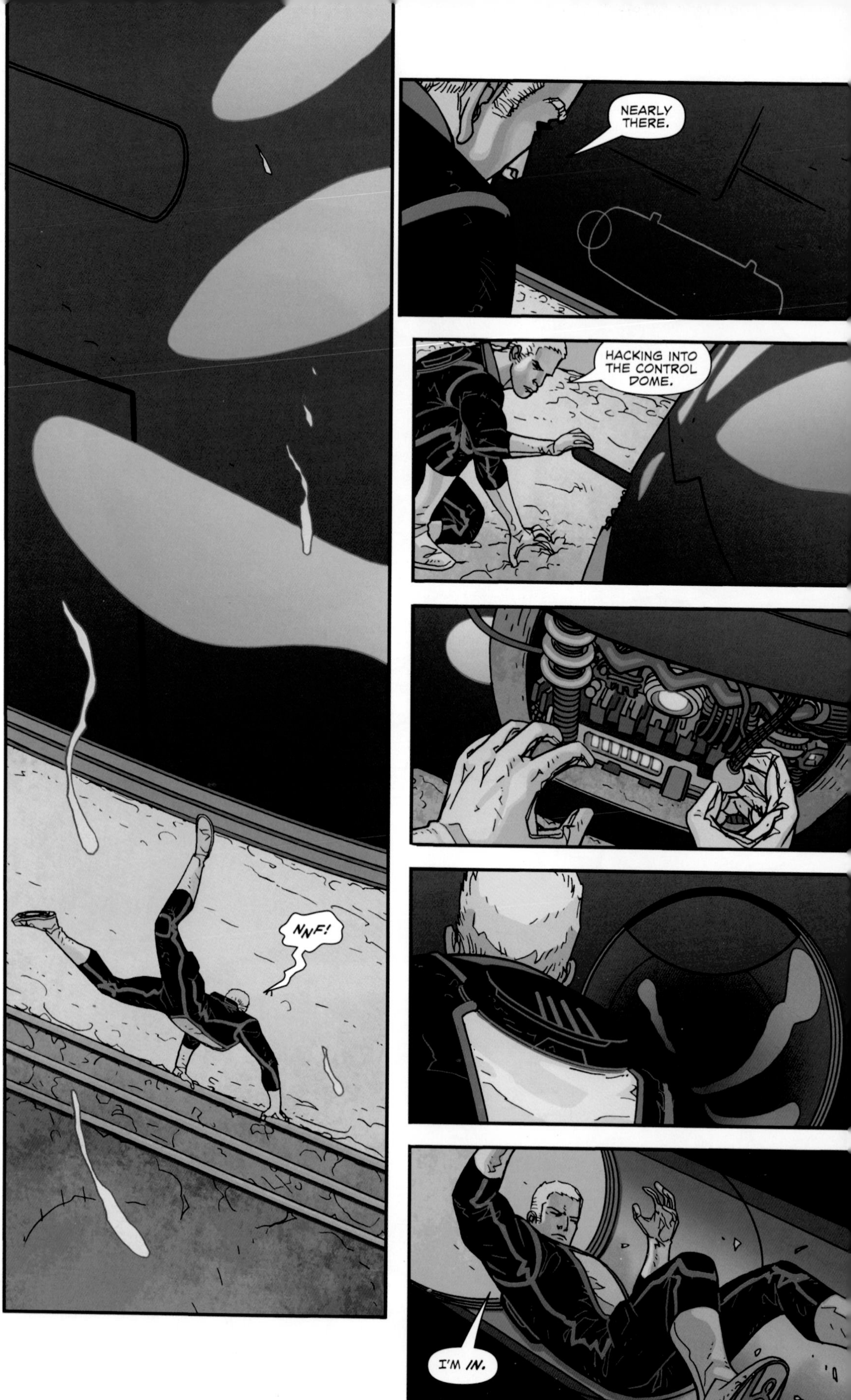

NNF!

NEARLY THERE.

HACKING INTO THE CONTROL DOME.

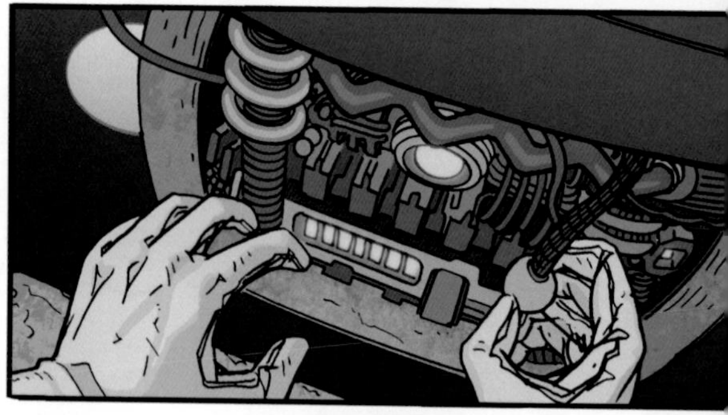

I'M *IN*.

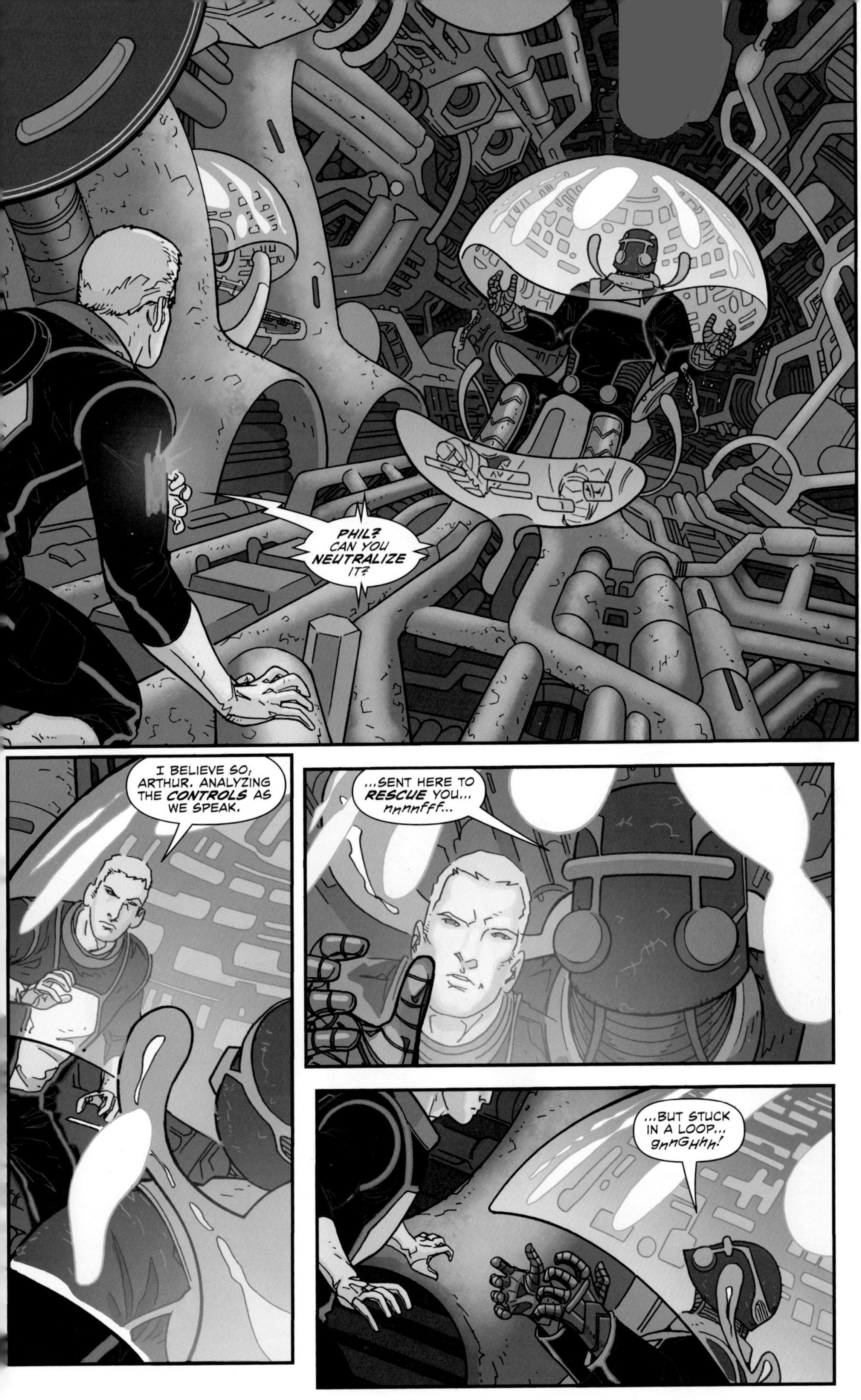

PHIL? CAN YOU NEUTRALIZE IT?

I BELIEVE SO, ARTHUR. ANALYZING THE CONTROLS AS WE SPEAK.

...SENT HERE TO RESCUE YOU... nnnnfff...

...BUT STUCK IN A LOOP... gnnGHhh!

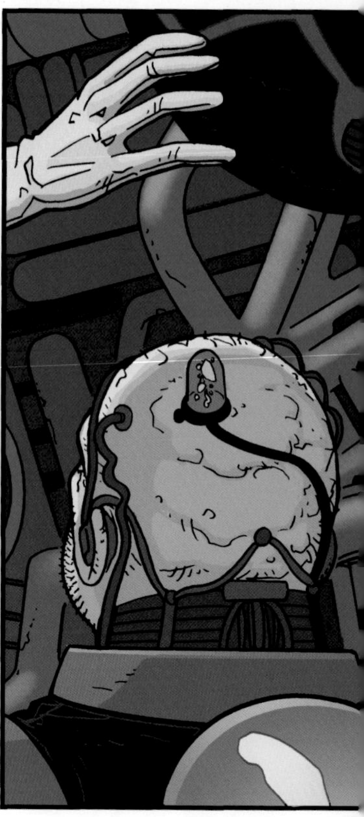

...YOU SEE? I WAS SENT HERE TO ***BRING YOU ALL HOME!*** BUT I CAN'T...THE SHIP WAS DAMAGED! AND SOMETHING IS ***WRONG*** WITH ME...

I KEEP REPEATING THE SAME TWENTY MINUTES... OVER AND OVER AGAIN. WE BATTLE, YOU RUIN MY SHIP, AND THEN IT ALL STARTS OVER AGAIN.
IT'S TIME SICKNESS. HAVE YOU SEEN ME BEFORE, OR IS THIS THE FIRST TIME WE'VE TALKED?
THE...FIRST... YES...YOU'VE DONE IT! YOU'VE BROKEN THE LOOP!
ONLY TEMPORARILY. BUT I THINK I CAN HELP YOU...HOLD ON. WHAT'S YOUR NAME?

HEIN... TROOPER HEIN...
OKAY, HEIN. HOLD ON...I'M GOING TO GET YOU OUT OF HERE.

BZZSHHHHH

PHIL? YOU OKAY?

YES, ARTHUR.

Portable transfer web capable of short-range teleportation. Illegal in all timelines.

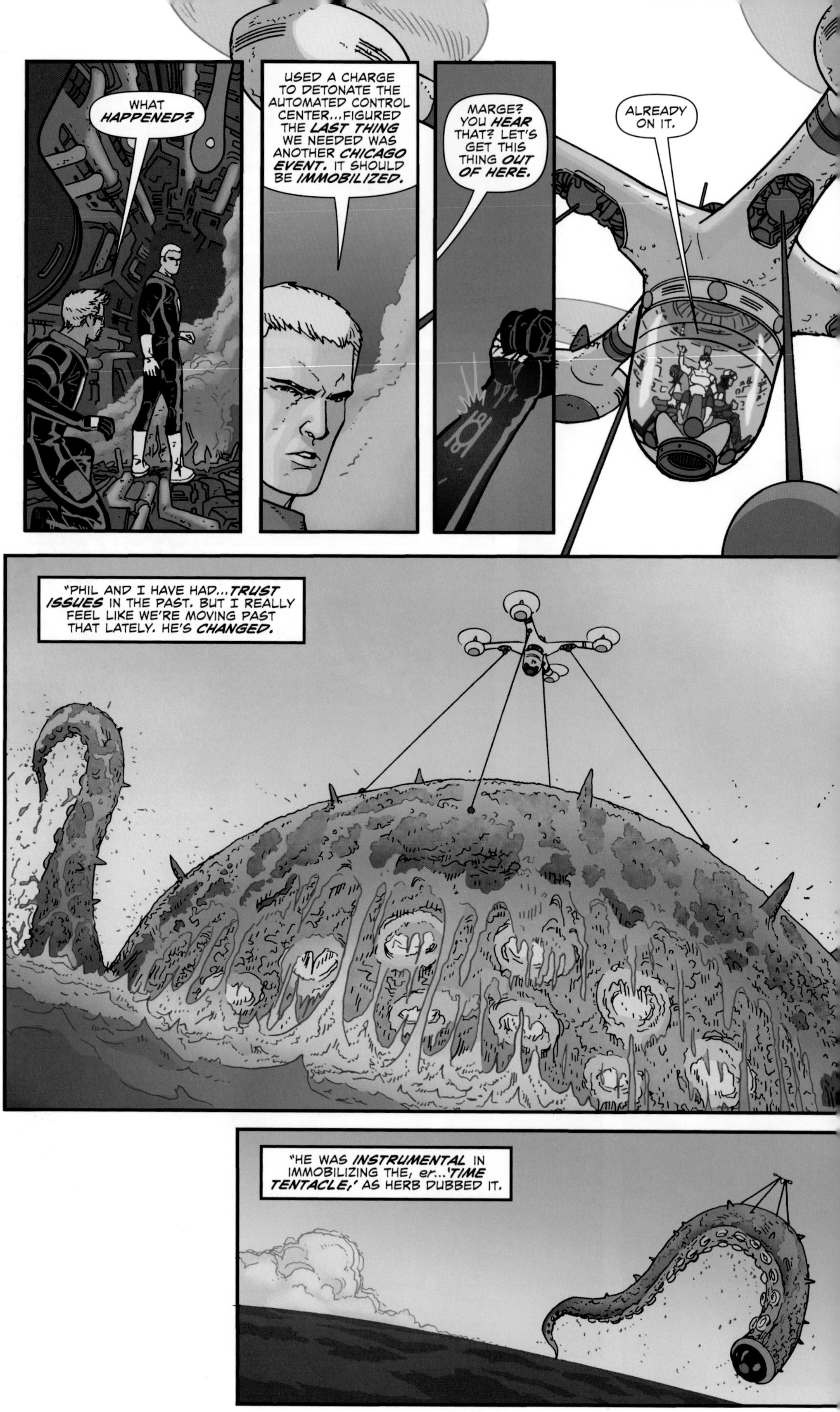

WHAT HAPPENED?
USED A CHARGE TO DETONATE THE AUTOMATED CONTROL CENTER...FIGURED THE LAST THING WE NEEDED WAS ANOTHER CHICAGO EVENT. IT SHOULD BE IMMOBILIZED.
MARGE? YOU HEAR THAT? LET'S GET THIS THING OUT OF HERE.
ALREADY ON IT.
"PHIL AND I HAVE HAD...TRUST ISSUES IN THE PAST. BUT I REALLY FEEL LIKE WE'RE MOVING PAST THAT LATELY. HE'S CHANGED.

"HE WAS INSTRUMENTAL IN IMMOBILIZING THE, er...'TIME TENTACLE,' AS HERB DUBBED IT.

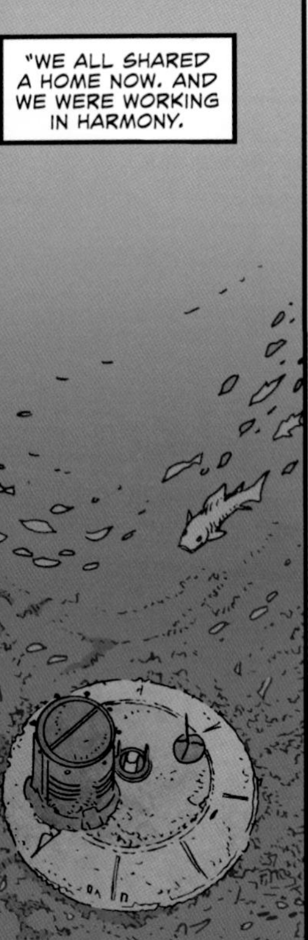
"WE ALL SHARED A HOME NOW. AND WE WERE WORKING IN HARMONY.

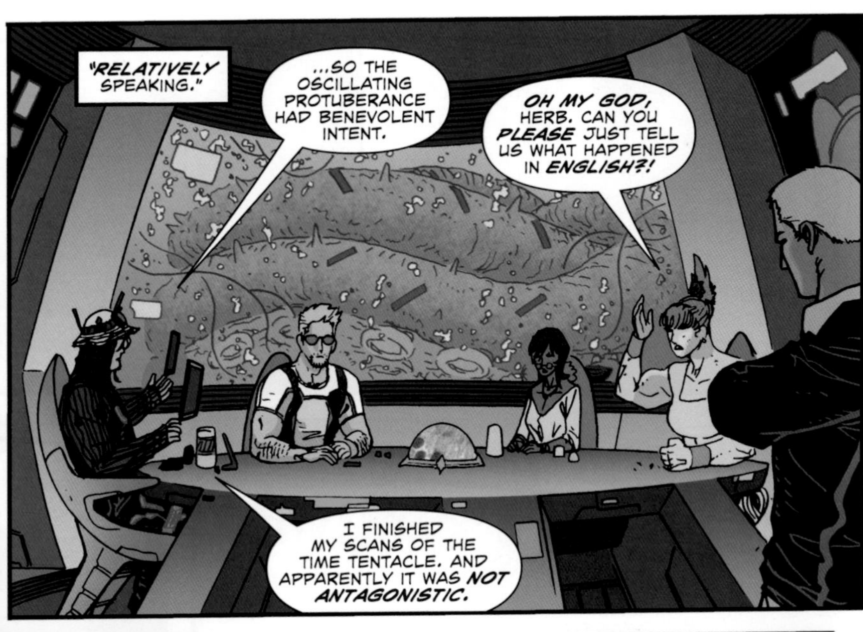
"RELATIVELY SPEAKING."
...SO THE OSCILLATING PROTUBERANCE HAD BENEVOLENT INTENT.
OH MY GOD, HERB. CAN YOU PLEASE JUST TELL US WHAT HAPPENED IN ENGLISH?!
I FINISHED MY SCANS OF THE TIME TENTACLE. AND APPARENTLY IT WAS NOT ANTAGONISTIC.

THE SURFACE OF THE TENTACLE IS COVERED WITH A MULTITUDE OF SPECIALIZED SATELLITE DISHES MEANT TO FIND US.
I BELIEVE IT IS... WELL...WAS ACTUALLY A RESCUE VESSEL.
SO YOU'RE TELLING ME WE JUST WRECKED OUR WAY BACK HOME? WONDERFUL.
WE BEEN HERE A FLIPPIN' YEAR AND WE FINALLY GET A WAY BACK, AND YOU DESTROY IT.

WELL, TECHNICALLY, PHIL DESTROYED THE CONTROL CENTER, BUT--
HE WAS ACTING UNDER MY ORDERS. DON'T BLAME HIM...

SO LET'S BLAME YOU, THEN, ART. YOU BROUGHT US ALL BACK TOGETHER WITH THE IDEA WE WERE GOING TO FIND A WAY HOME. AND THEN YOU INADVERTENTLY RUINED IT.

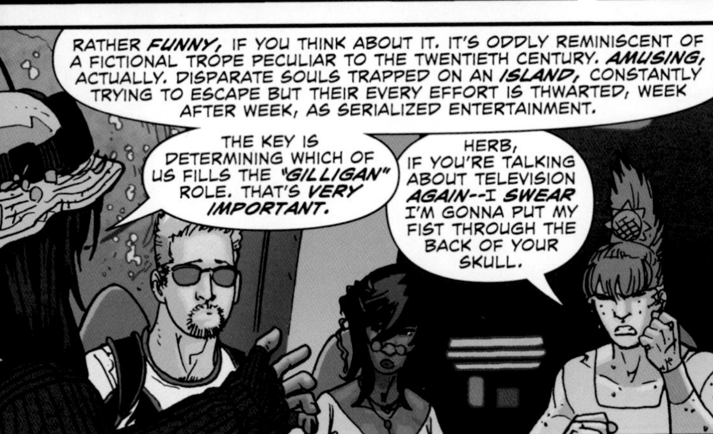
RATHER FUNNY, IF YOU THINK ABOUT IT. IT'S ODDLY REMINISCENT OF A FICTIONAL TROPE PECULIAR TO THE TWENTIETH CENTURY. AMUSING, ACTUALLY. DISPARATE SOULS TRAPPED ON AN ISLAND, CONSTANTLY TRYING TO ESCAPE BUT THEIR EVERY EFFORT IS THWARTED, WEEK AFTER WEEK, AS SERIALIZED ENTERTAINMENT.
THE KEY IS DETERMINING WHICH OF US FILLS THE "GILLIGAN" ROLE. THAT'S VERY IMPORTANT.
HERB, IF YOU'RE TALKING ABOUT TELEVISION AGAIN--I SWEAR I'M GONNA PUT MY FIST THROUGH THE BACK OF YOUR SKULL.
RATHER THAN ATTACK ME, IF YOU ALL WOULD TAKE MY SUGGESTION--AND IMMERSE YOURSELVES IN THE CULTURE OF OUR CURRENT ERA...YOU MIGHT FIND ACCLIMATION TO BE A BIT MORE... FACILE.

IT DOESN'T HAVE TO BE TELEVISION. IF YOU WOULD SIMPLY TAKE A WALK IN THE REAL WORLD RATHER THAN LIVE HOLED UP LIKE WE'VE BEEN--

YES. ABOUT THAT. ARE YOU SURE WE'RE NOT GOING TO GET SOME RIDICULOUS TWENTY-FIRST CENTURY DISEASE?
I'VE TOLD YOU. OUR MICROFILTER EXOSKINS ARE DESIGNED TO IMMUNIZE US INSTANTLY AND ADAPT TO ANY PATHOGEN.

PLUS, WE CAN'T DIE, URS. REMEMBER? "THE TIMESTREAM PROTECTS ITSELF," SO WE CAN'T DIE BEFORE WE WERE BORN.
WHICH IS RIDICULOUS, HERB. WHY WOULD TIME CARE ABOUT US?

WELL, THAT'S NOT EXACTLY WHAT I'M SAYING...

OUR INVULNERABILITY PROVES THAT SOMEONE IS LOOKING OUT FOR US. A HIGHER POWER THAT YOUR SCIENCE SIMPLY CAN'T EXPLAIN.

MARGE, PLEASE. BELIEVE WHAT YOU LIKE, BUT THE REST OF THE TEA WOULD PREFER YOU DON' CONTAMINATE OUR THOUGHT WITH IRRATIONA CONCEPTS.

EVERYONE! LET'S CALM DOWN FOR JUST A MINUTE. PLEASE...

I JUST...
I WANT TO APOLOGIZE. I WAS SUPPOSED TO BE THE LEADER, AND I'VE FAILED YOU. I WAS SUPPOSED TO PROTECT YOU. EVERYTHING WRONG THAT'S HAPPENED...IT'S ON MY SHOULDERS.
YOU HAVE ALL ACTED EXCEPTIONALLY.
IF ANYTHING, I HAVEN'T LIVED UP TO YOUR EXPECTATIONS.

WE WORK WELL TOGETHER BECAUSE OF OUR DIFFERENCES. WE ALL BRING SOMETHING DIFFERENT TO THE TABLE.
BUT WE SHARE SOMETHING AS WELL.

WE SIGNED UP FOR THIS MISSION BECAUSE WE WERE CURIOUS. WE WANTED KNOWLEDGE. WE WANTED TO SEE THE UNKNOWN. WE WANTED TO SEE FORGOTTEN SUNSETS AND EXPERIENCE LOST CIVILIZATIONS.
AND WE'RE DOING THAT.
WE'RE DOING WHAT WE CAME HERE TO DO. SO LET'S KEEP DOING IT.
AND EVENTUALLY... I PROMISE YOU ALL--

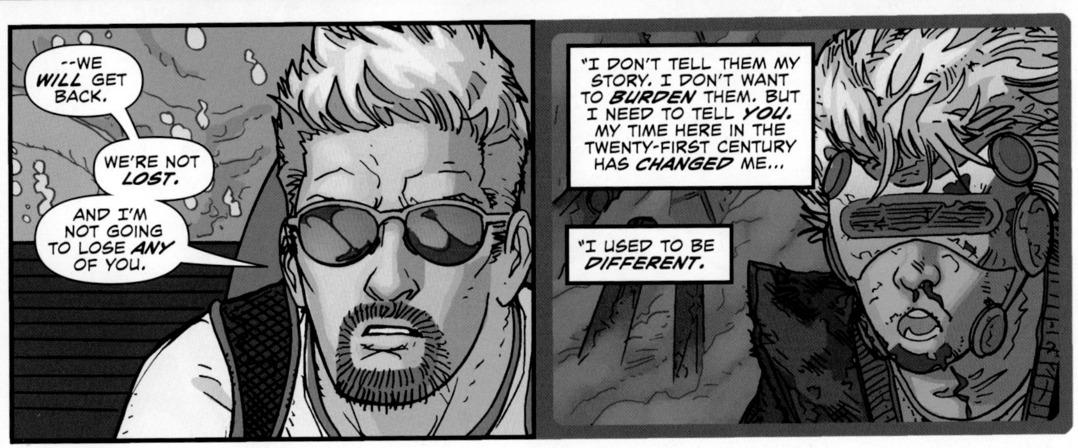
--WE WILL GET BACK.
WE'RE NOT LOST.
AND I'M NOT GOING TO LOSE ANY OF YOU.
"I DON'T TELL THEM MY STORY. I DON'T WANT TO BURDEN THEM. BUT I NEED TO TELL YOU. MY TIME HERE IN THE TWENTY-FIRST CENTURY HAS CHANGED ME...
"I USED TO BE DIFFERENT.

"I WORKED A MINING VESSEL WITH MY FAMILY.

"I WAS THIRTEEN WHEN THE SHIP SUFFERED A CATASTROPHIC SERIES OF MECHANICAL FAILURES.

"I LOST MY ENTIRE FAMILY. I WAS ALONE.
"STRANDED ON AN ALIEN PLANET THAT HAD ONCE BEEN INHABITED BY CURRILIAN MONKS.

"AFTER A FEW MONTHS, I REALIZED THAT NO ONE WAS COMING TO HELP ME. FATE WAS NOT GOING TO INTERVENE.
"I HAD TO DO IT ON MY OWN...

"AND, ON MY OWN, I BUILT A PATCHWORK SHIP THAT GOT ME OFF THAT DESOLATE PLANET.

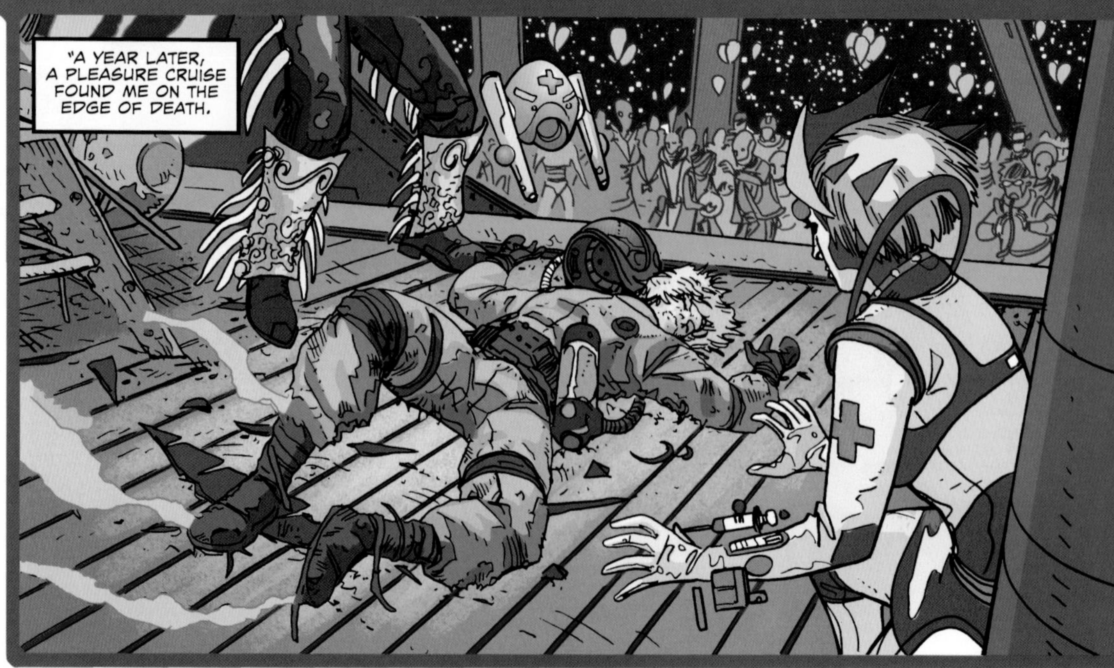
"A YEAR LATER, A PLEASURE CRUISE FOUND ME ON THE EDGE OF DEATH.

"FIVE YEARS LATER, I WAS THE YOUNGEST-EVER PRESIDENT OF THE LARGEST MINING OPERATION ON MARS.
"MARS WAS A DIRTY PLACE. FULL OF CORRUPT POLITICIANS AND BUILT ON A BEDROCK OF ORGANIZED CRIME AND SLAVE LABOR.
"IT WASN'T A PLANET FOR THE FAINT OF HEART."
HAHA HA!
MAKE HIM BLEED!

"THAT'S WHERE I MET PHIL."
STOP IT!
GET OUT OF HERE!

GO ON!
BZZZT
...WHY... WHY...?
WHY DID YOU INTERVENE?...YOU CAN SEE WHAT I AM...NOT ONE...OF YOU. NOT EVEN HUMAN. I'M A... NO-SOUL.
I DON'T BELIEVE IN SOULS, PARTNER.
AND I DON'T BELIEVE IN TORTURE, EITHER.

☐ Defensive smart water laced with nanoranhas to stave off intruders.

"THAT'S WHY I'M *HERE.* PHIL TOLD ME ABOUT YOU. TOLD ME THAT IT MIGHT HELP... TO *TALK* TO SOMEONE.

"SOMEONE OUTSIDE THE TEAM. TO TELL THEM MY STORY.

"SOMEONE FROM *THIS ERA.* SOMEONE... *NORMAL.*"

IF YOU DIDN'T BEFORE, I'M SURE YOU THINK I'M CRAZY NOW.

NO, ART.

I... I *BELIEVE* YOU.

WHAT ARE YOU DOING TO ME?
Improvised stealth shed constructed with blue solar panels and designed with environment-spoofing cameras. Invisible to the human eye.

I'M HELPING YOU.

I'LL KEEP FIXING YOUR TIME SICKNESS...

BUT IN RETURN...

ART NEEDS TO DIE.

HERBERT TRAVELOGUE

November 2014.

Once again, I embarked on an interesting interaction unique to the *twenty-first century* (to use the local time/date vernacular). It is no longer shocking to observe the crude technological "achievements" of this era and, to some degree, I think that I am, and we as a team are, adjusting marvelously. Whether it be the slower-than-sound modes of transportation or the simple lack of sentient stairwells, our minds are slowly adjusting to the limits that our predicament places on us.

We have worked diligently to create a headquarters that, at least superficially, seems to feel like home, with some of the basic comforts. But outside of our team domicile, the world is still a strange and threatening place. Our team leader, Arthur, recently visited what is known in this era as a psychologist. Interestingly enough, he went at the recommendation of Philip. I'm consistently amazed at the strides in integration and normalization that nonhuman constructs have made over the years, and Phil is an impeccable example.

But I digress. I thought that visiting a vintage-era psychologist would be a worthy endeavor to experience and document. I couldn't have been further from the truth. As I entered the psychologist's "operating room," I was struck by the unprofessional and "cozy" demeanor (to borrow a contemporary phrase) of the facility. It literally looked like the "doctor" was operating out of her living room and I'm not quite convinced that this *wasn't* the case.

I went in with the simple objective of receiving some general mental health maintenance. But instead of being met by a series of six-dimensional scanners and a battery of mind diodes to assess my current condition, I was simply placed in a chair, asked a series of basic questions, and invited to talk about my "issues." There were no gray-matter minidrones or neural spider crawlers to actually go in and take a look at whatever issues might be troubling me.

After an hour of being encouraged to talk and prattle on and on, I finally had had enough and called an end to the entire pointless affair. Admittedly, I did grow a little angry as I left and the psychologist flash-diagnosed me with chronic anger and anxiety issues, along with unchecked feelings of abandonment and fear of failure. Her diagnosis was still echoing in my ears as I stormed out of the session and returned to the more familiar confines of our headquarters.

It wasn't until I returned "home" that I realized that, even with her crude process and outmoded technical knowledge . . . her diagnosis was profoundly correct.

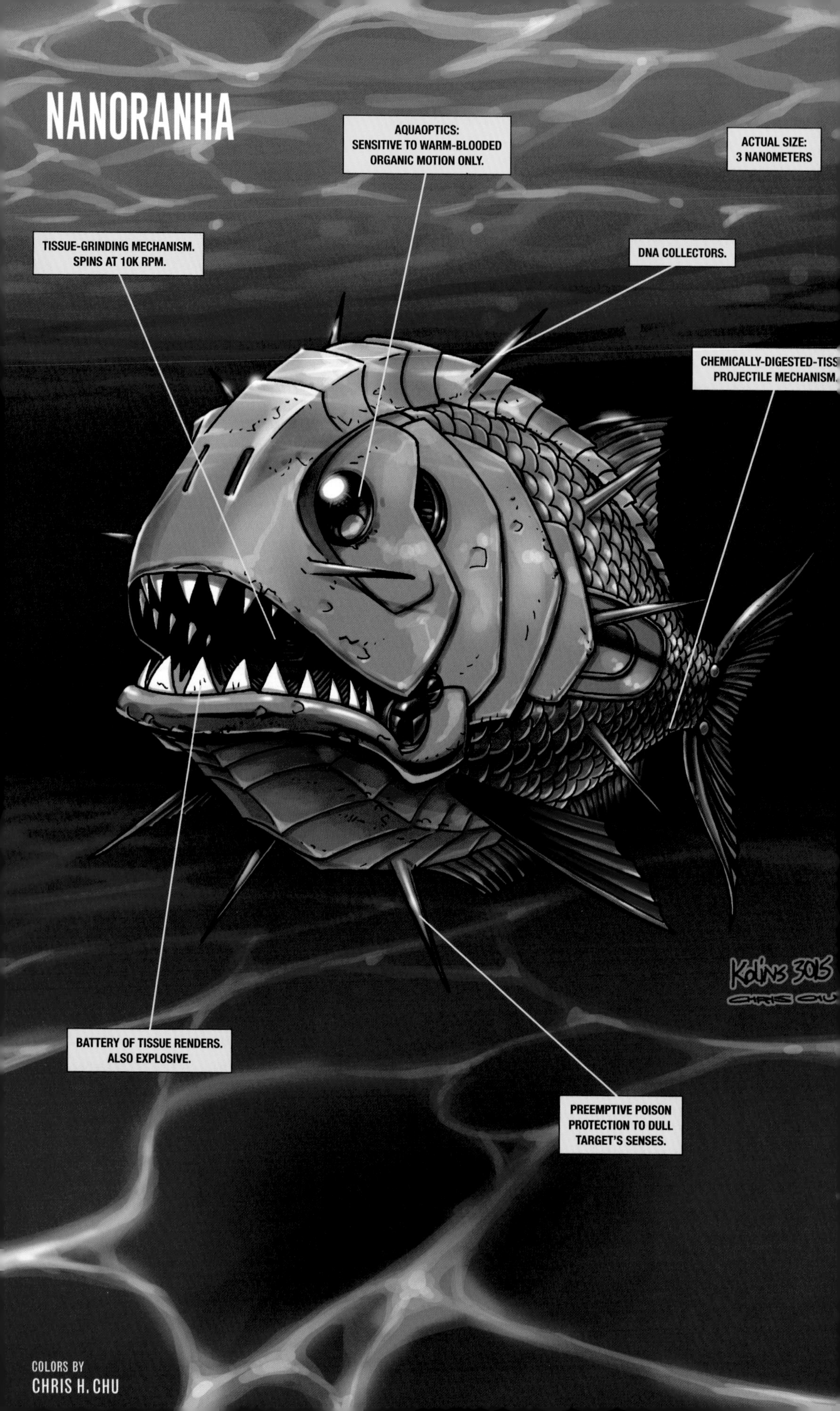

NANOROANHA

AQUAOPTICS:
SENSITIVE TO WARM-BLOODED ORGANIC MOTION ONLY.

ACTUAL SIZE:
3 NANOMETERS

TISSUE-GRINDING MECHANISM.
SPINS AT 10K RPM.

DNA COLLECTORS.

CHEMICALLY-DIGESTED-TISS
PROJECTILE MECHANISM.

BATTERY OF TISSUE RENDERS.
ALSO EXPLOSIVE.

PREEMPTIVE POISON PROTECTION TO DULL TARGET'S SENSES.

COLORS BY
CHRIS H. CHU

PAST AWAYS
MATT KINDT SCOTT KOLINS
BILL CRABTREE

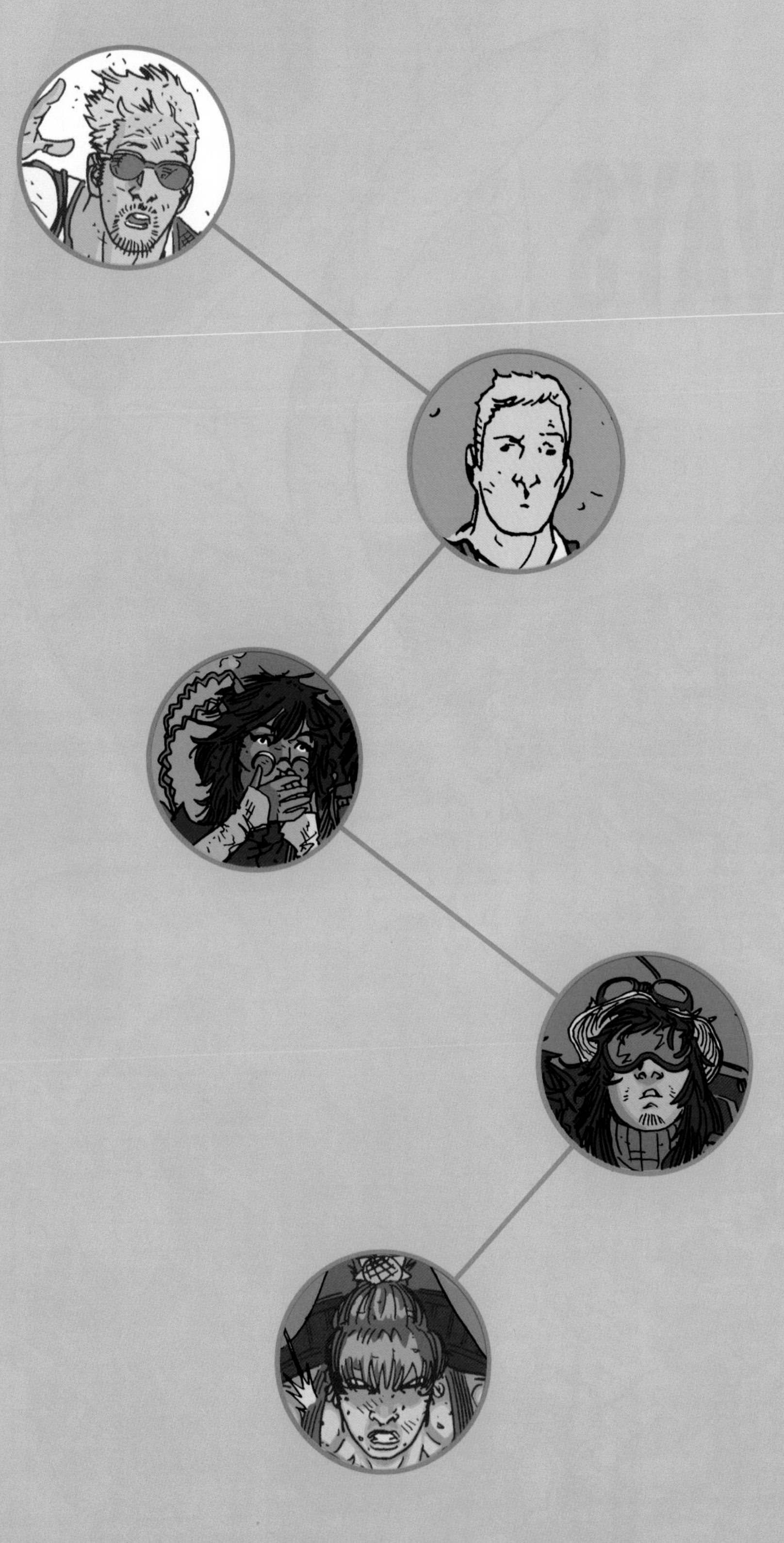

I COULD INSTANTLY TRANSPORT YOU TO YOUR DESIRED LEVEL IF YOU'D LIKE, PHIL.
NO, THANK YOU. I PREFER TO WALK.

AS YOU WISH, SIR. WOULD YOU LIKE ME TO ALERT YOU WHEN YOU'VE ARRIVED?
NOT NECESSARY. YOU'RE CLEARLY LABELED.
OF COURSE.

I'M CURIOUS... DO I CALL YOU... "STAIRS"?
CERTAINLY, SIR. I ANSWER TO STAIRCASE, STAIRS, VERTICAL INGRESS, PORT, PORTAL, AND SEVERAL THOUSAND MORE ITERATIONS.
THANK YOU. HOW LONG HAVE YOU BEEN SELF-AWARE?

APPROXIMATELY SIX MONTHS, SIR. EVER SINCE YOUR TEAMMATES ARTHUR AND HERBERT INSTALLED ME AND BROUGHT ME ONLINE.
DO YOU REMEMBER WHERE YOU CAME FROM?
WHY, YES, SIR. I WAS ORIGINALLY INSTALLED AS PART OF A SPACE ELEVATOR IN THE YEAR 39B. A TIME POCKET FORMED AROUND ME SOON AFTER AND I FOUND MYSELF TRANSPORTED TO THE TWENTY-FIRST CENTURY. ARTHUR FOUND ME FLOATING IN THE OCEAN AND RESCUED ME.
INTERESTING.

CAN YOU TELL ME WHAT'S GOING ON AT LEVEL THREE, STAIRS?
YES, SIR. IT APPEARS AS IF THE VENOMOUS TORTOISE IN THE TROPHY ROOM HAS BECOME REANIMATED AND IS CURRENTLY TRYING TO ESCAPE.
3

OH, *GOOD LORD.* ART AND HIS *TROPHY ROOMS.*

Shcorpio is an automaton predator built for home security nearly one thousand years from now. Considered a failure by tech-industry standards, as it lacked lethal capabilities and had an adorable voice that children loved.

TORTOISE PACKS A *WALLOP*...
≈cough cough≈
NnNgh! GIVE ME A MINUTE AND I'LL HAVE THIS THING *BEGGING* FOR MERCY!
IS THE NEW BATTERY IN YET, URSULA?!
I'M WORKING AS *FAST* AS I CAN.

I TOLD YOU THE TORPOR TUBES WERE UNSTABLE, ART. IT WASN'T GOING TO STAY ASLEEP FOREVER.
ONE MORE BLAST SHOULD DO IT...!
AAAHHHG! HERB, YOU GODLESS HEATHEN! YOU'RE HITTING ME!
CUT THE POWER, HERB-- YOU'RE CATCHING MARGE IN THE CROSSFIRE!
Nnngh...
HERB... JUST CUT IT OUT...YOU'RE ONLY...

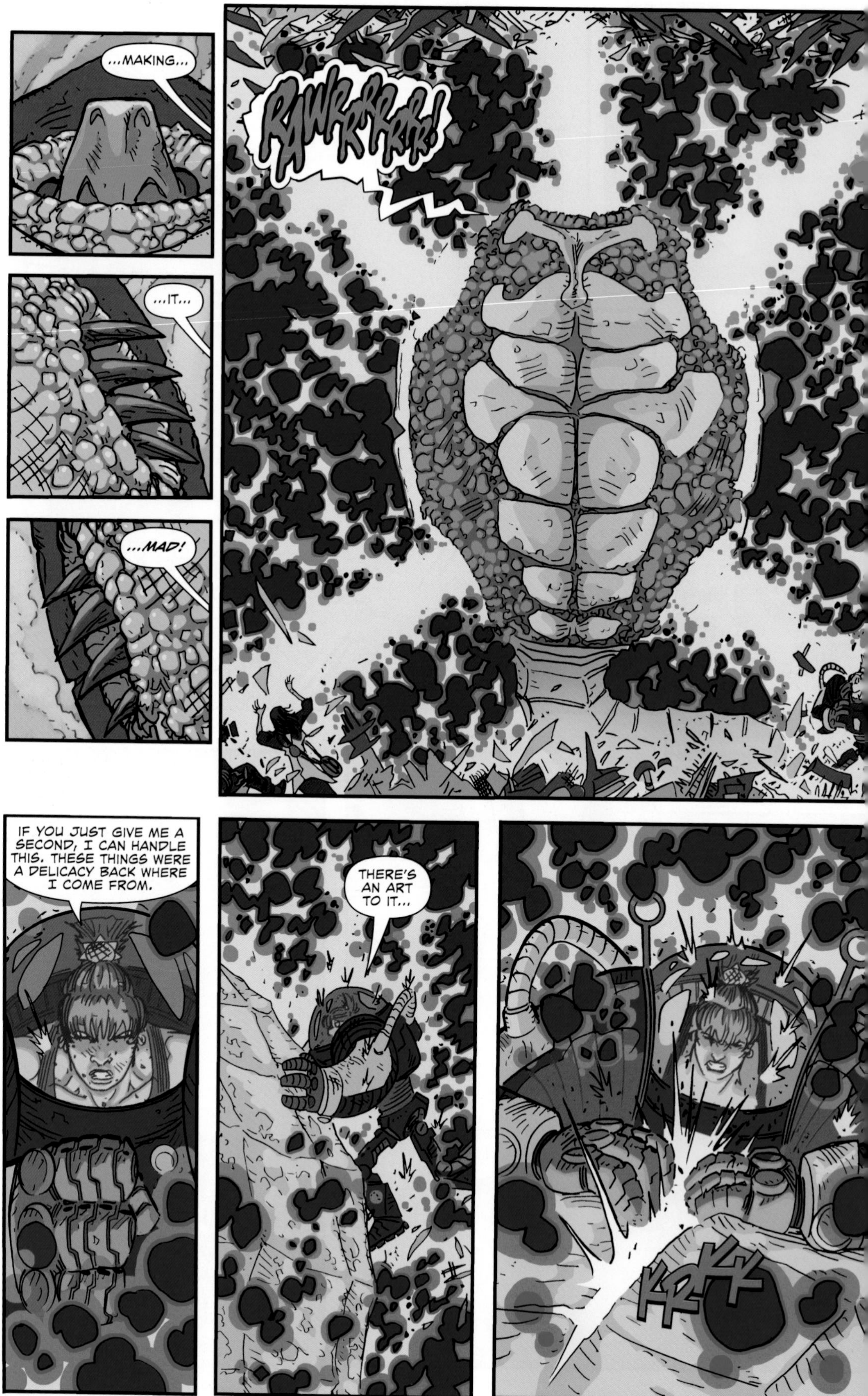

...MAKING...

...IT...

...MAD!

IF YOU JUST GIVE ME A SECOND, I CAN HANDLE THIS. THESE THINGS WERE A DELICACY BACK WHERE I COME FROM.

THERE'S AN ART TO IT...

MARGE, ARE YOU SURE...?!
OH GODS...
NO... NO...
I... I...
...SUCH A... SUCH A WASTE...

I'LL BE *DAMNED.*

THING WAS *PREGNANT.*

BETTER GET THESE EGGS UP BEFORE THEY *HATCH.* I'M GOING TO CLEAN UP.

ART--! WE NEED A CONTAINMENT CRATE NOW!

Shew! YOU SURE THEY'RE *ALIVE?* THEY DON'T *SMELL* ALIVE.
I'M SURE, ART. AND THEY GROW *EXPONENTIALLY.* ONCE THEY HATCH, WE'VE GOT ABOUT *THIRTY-SIX HOURS* BEFORE THEY REACH THEIR FULL SIZE. AND THERE ARE *HUNDREDS* OF THEM!

URSULA, PHIL! GET TO THE SUPPLY ROOM. THERE'S A CONTAINMENT CRATE THERE. HAVE THE STAIRS BRING IT DOWN RIGHT AWAY.
ON IT.

Automated cleaning robot equipped with nanodisintegration chemicals capable of tackling the largest of messes. Currently, it is overwhelmed.

AUTHOR
PERSON
ONLY
The Chihuahuan Desert. Southern New Mexico.
8:30 a.m.

8:31 (and 29 seconds) a.m.

8:31 (and 35 seconds) a.m.

8:31 (and 29 seconds) a.m.

8:31 (and 35 seconds) a.m.

8:35 (and 45 seconds) a.m.

8:35 (and 50 seconds) a.m.

8:35 (and 45 seconds) a.m.

8:35 (and 50 seconds) a.m.

Somewhere over Chile.
TRUST ME, ART.
THIS PLACE IS PERFECT. IT'S A ONE-WAY TIME TEAR. I FOUND IT WHEN WE WERE... NOT TALKING. IT'S A HOLE IN TIME THAT'S BEEN HERE FOR HUNDREDS OF YEARS. I THINK THE MAYANS CAPPED IT SOMEHOW.
I TRUST YOU, PHIL. IT'S A GOOD FIND.
IT'S... BEAUTIFUL.

Containment crate autoscans and catalogs contents and uploads to the Neither-Net for postadventure review.

READINGS ARE ALL OFF THE CHART. WHICH IS *NORMAL.*

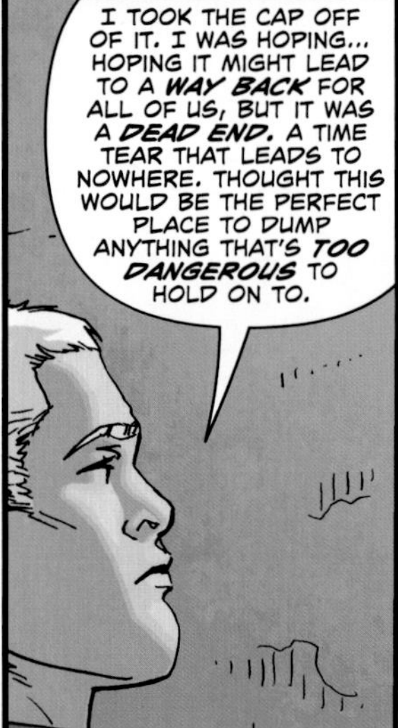

I TOOK THE CAP OFF OF IT. I WAS HOPING... HOPING IT MIGHT LEAD TO A *WAY BACK* FOR ALL OF US, BUT IT WAS A *DEAD END.* A TIME TEAR THAT LEADS TO NOWHERE. THOUGHT THIS WOULD BE THE PERFECT PLACE TO DUMP ANYTHING THAT'S *TOO DANGEROUS* TO HOLD ON TO.

SCANNING NOW, ART... AND PHIL IS *RIGHT.* SEEMS LIKE THE MAYANS EITHER *STUMBLED UPON* OR *UNWITTINGLY OPENED* A PORTAL TO THE *UNTIMES.*

THERE'S SOME STRANGE INTERFERENCE OVER THE TOP OF IT THOUGH. CAN'T QUITE READ IT. LIKE THERE'S A FILTER ON IT.

☐ Goggles equipped with intelligent-designed floating lenses that adapt to the environment and predict the user's needs based on audio-visual cl

YOU THINK 'S SAFE TO JUST PUMP THE EGGS IN THERE?
I'D LIKE TO DO A FEW MORE SCANS. RUN SOME TESTS...

MAYBE RUN A *TRIAL POD* THROUGH IT FIRST AND BRING IT BACK. MAKE SURE IT'S NOT JUST *POPPING UP* IN ANOTHER REALITY.

I HAVEN'T SEEN A *NATURALLY OCCURRING* UNTIME PORTAL BEFORE. IN THEORY ALL OF THEM SHOULD LEAD TO THE *NO-ZONE,* WHERE THINGS SIMPLY *STOP EXISTING.* NEVER WERE. NEVER ARE AGAIN. BUT IN OUR TIMES, ACCESS WAS NATURALLY *RESTRICTED.*

IT WILL BE OKAY, HERB. *TRUST ME.* I SPENT A LOT OF TIME DOWN HERE STUDYING IT. I SENT SEVERAL TRIAL PODS IN MYSELF. ALL THE *MICROFEEDBACK* I RECEIVED WAS POSITIVE. IT'S *SAFE.*

IT'S NOT THAT I DON'T TRUST YOU, PHIL. IT'S JUST... UNTIME PORTALS ARE STILL A RELATIVELY *UNKNOWN QUANTITY.* NO ONE HAS EVER REALLY DOCUMENTED WHAT HAPPENS. THERE'S MASS AND MATTER DISPLACEMENT TO WORRY ABOUT. HOW DOES OUR REALITY *BALANCE OUT* THE LOSS OF REALITY MATTER? FINE ON A SMALL SCALE, BUT IF WE DROP SOMETHING LIKE A *GIANT CRATE OF EGGS* INTO IT, THERE'S NO TELLING--

WHADAYAKNOW?
IT WORKS.

OH MY...!
WELL, THAT ANSWERS THAT.

OKAY, TEAM. WE'RE DONE HERE. TAKE A FEW MINUTES. LET'S SEARCH THE AREA FOR ANOMALIES AND THEN WE'LL GET BACK HOME.

IT FEELS GOOD, PHIL. I'M GLAD WE'RE WORKING TOGETHER AGAIN.
I APPRECIATE THE TRUST, ART.

YOU'RE NOT WORRIED ABOUT LEAVING THE HEADQUARTERS UNATTENDED FOR THIS LONG?

NO, NO. IT'LL BE OKAY. OTHER THAN THE ODD TROPHY ROOM ITEM PERKING UP HERE AND THERE. IT'S IMPERVIOUS TO OUTSIDE INTRUDERS. TRUST ME.

"I HIRED A TEAM OF END-OF-THE-WORLD SURVIVALISTS TO BE AN EARLY WARNING SYSTEM FOR US.

"THEY'RE A *HARDENED* GROUP. MOST OF THEM ARE EX-MILITARY.

"I FEEL BAD FOR ANYONE WHO TRIES TO GET BY THEM."

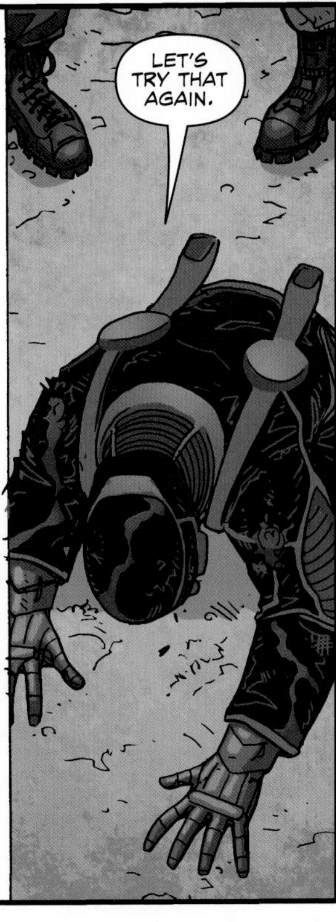
LET'S TRY THAT AGAIN.

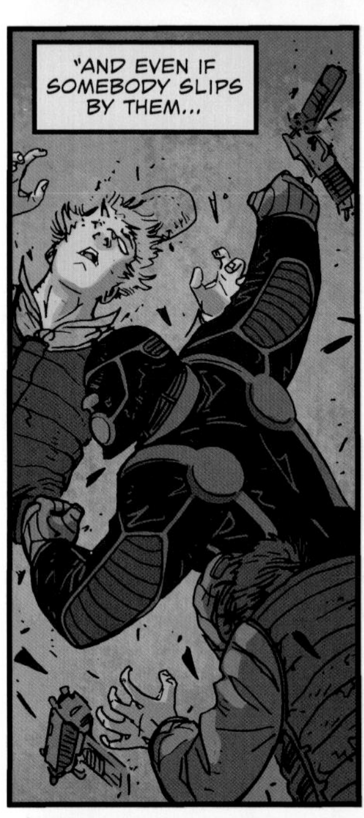
"AND EVEN IF SOMEBODY SLIPS BY THEM...

"...SHORT OF A HIGH-LEVEL MILITARY OPERATION, NO ONE IS GOING TO JUST ROLL OVER THEM."

ONE MORE TIME OUGHTA DO IT.

"I GAVE THEM A PANIC BUTTON IN THE UNLIKELY EVENT THAT SOMEONE OR SOME *THING* DOES GET BY THEM.

"AFTER THAT, ANYONE LOOKING FOR OUR HEADQUARTERS WILL STILL HAVE TO *FIND* IT.

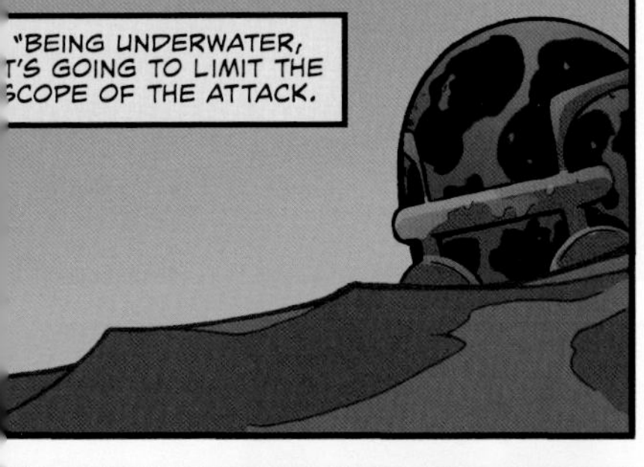
"BEING UNDERWATER, IT'S GOING TO LIMIT THE SCOPE OF THE ATTACK.

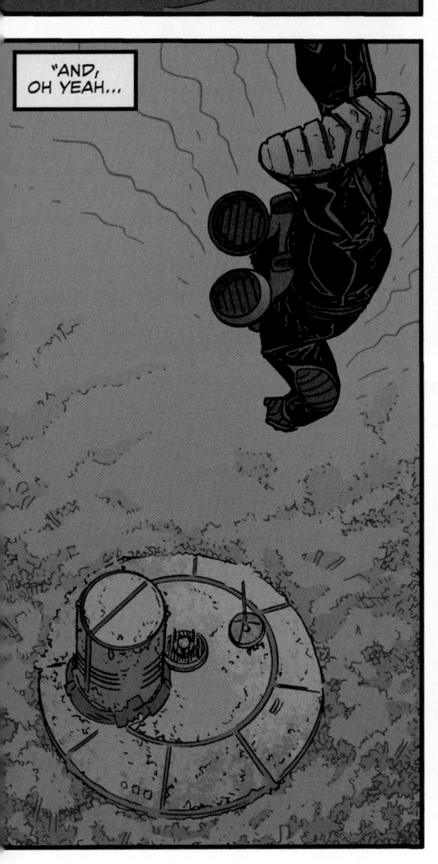
"AND, OH YEAH...

"I STOCKED THE LAKE WITH FLESH-EATING *NANORANHAS.*

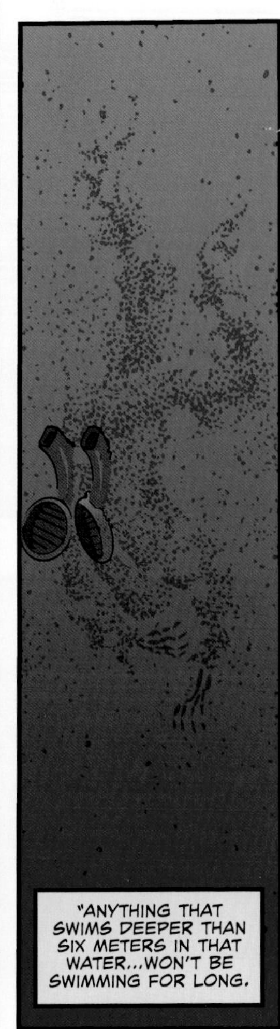
"ANYTHING THAT SWIMS DEEPER THAN SIX METERS IN THAT WATER...WON'T BE SWIMMING FOR LONG.

"IT'S MORE THAN A HEADQUARTERS, PHIL.
SHOCK DROPS SHOULD DO THE JOB.
"THAT BASE IS OUR SANCTUM."

"IT'S THE ONE PLACE WE CAN ALL RELAX.
"IT'S EASY NOW. NO ONE REALLY KNOWS WHO WE ARE YET. WE AVOIDED GOING PUBLIC.

"BUT IT MIGHT NOT ALWAYS BE THAT WAY. HECK, AFTER CHICAGO, I THOUGHT WE WOULD HAVE TO GO PUBLIC.
"SO THAT HQ IS VITAL FOR OUR SURVIVAL.

"AS A TEAM. AS A FAMILY.

"THAT HEADQUARTERS IS HOME, PHIL. HOME TO ALL OF US.
"UNTIL WE CAN GET BACK TO OUR TIME. IT'S ALL WE'VE GOT."

☐ Shock drops, a.k.a. Duce Makinaws, are commonly used as a passive form of poison and are microloaded with every conceivable form of poison and a microprinter. They are capable, on the fly, of manufacturing the perfect lethal answer to any problem.

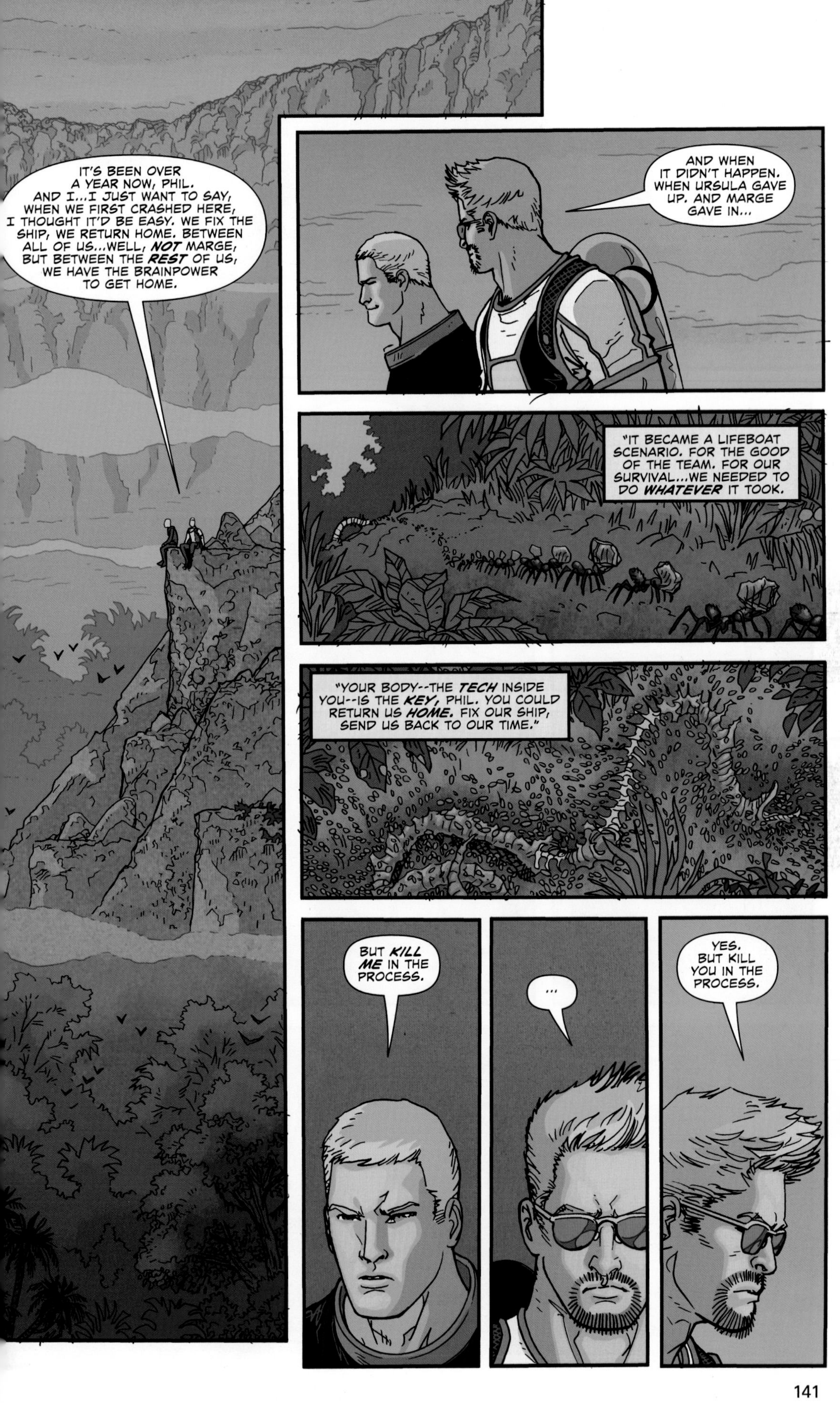
IT'S BEEN OVER A YEAR NOW, PHIL. AND I...I JUST WANT TO SAY, WHEN WE FIRST CRASHED HERE, I THOUGHT IT'D BE EASY. WE FIX THE SHIP, WE RETURN HOME. BETWEEN ALL OF US...WELL, NOT MARGE, BUT BETWEEN THE REST OF US, WE HAVE THE BRAINPOWER TO GET HOME.
AND WHEN IT DIDN'T HAPPEN. WHEN URSULA GAVE UP. AND MARGE GAVE IN...
"IT BECAME A LIFEBOAT SCENARIO. FOR THE GOOD OF THE TEAM. FOR OUR SURVIVAL...WE NEEDED TO DO WHATEVER IT TOOK.
"YOUR BODY--THE TECH INSIDE YOU--IS THE KEY, PHIL. YOU COULD RETURN US HOME. FIX OUR SHIP, SEND US BACK TO OUR TIME."
BUT KILL ME IN THE PROCESS.
...
YES. BUT KILL YOU IN THE PROCESS.

I WAS WILLING TO SACRIFICE YOUR LIFE FOR THE GOOD OF THE TEAM, PHIL. JUST AS I WOULD SACRIFICE *MINE.* IN A HEARTBEAT.

BUT JUST BECAUSE *I* WOULD BE WILLING TO MAKE THAT SACRIFICE, I GUESS...I EXPECTED YOU TO BE WILLING TO DO THE SAME.

I'M DIFFERENT THAN YOU, ART. I BELIEVE THERE IS A WAY TO GET BACK *WITHOUT* ME SACRIFICING MY LIFE.

I KNOW. I KNOW YOU'RE RIGHT NOW, PHIL. AND WE'LL DO IT. WE *WILL.* WE'RE GOING TO DO IT THE RIGHT WAY.

PLUS, WE CAN'T DIE ANYWAY. RIGHT? OR DO YOU BELIEVE SINCE I'M...ARTIFICIAL, THAT MY DEATH WOULD NOT CAUSE A CONUNDRUM? THAT TIME DOES NOT *PROTECT* ME?

IT PROTECTS YOU, PHIL. IT PROTECTS *US ALL.*

FOR BETTER OR WORSE, *eh?*

NO, PHIL. FOR BETTER. FOR *BETTER.*

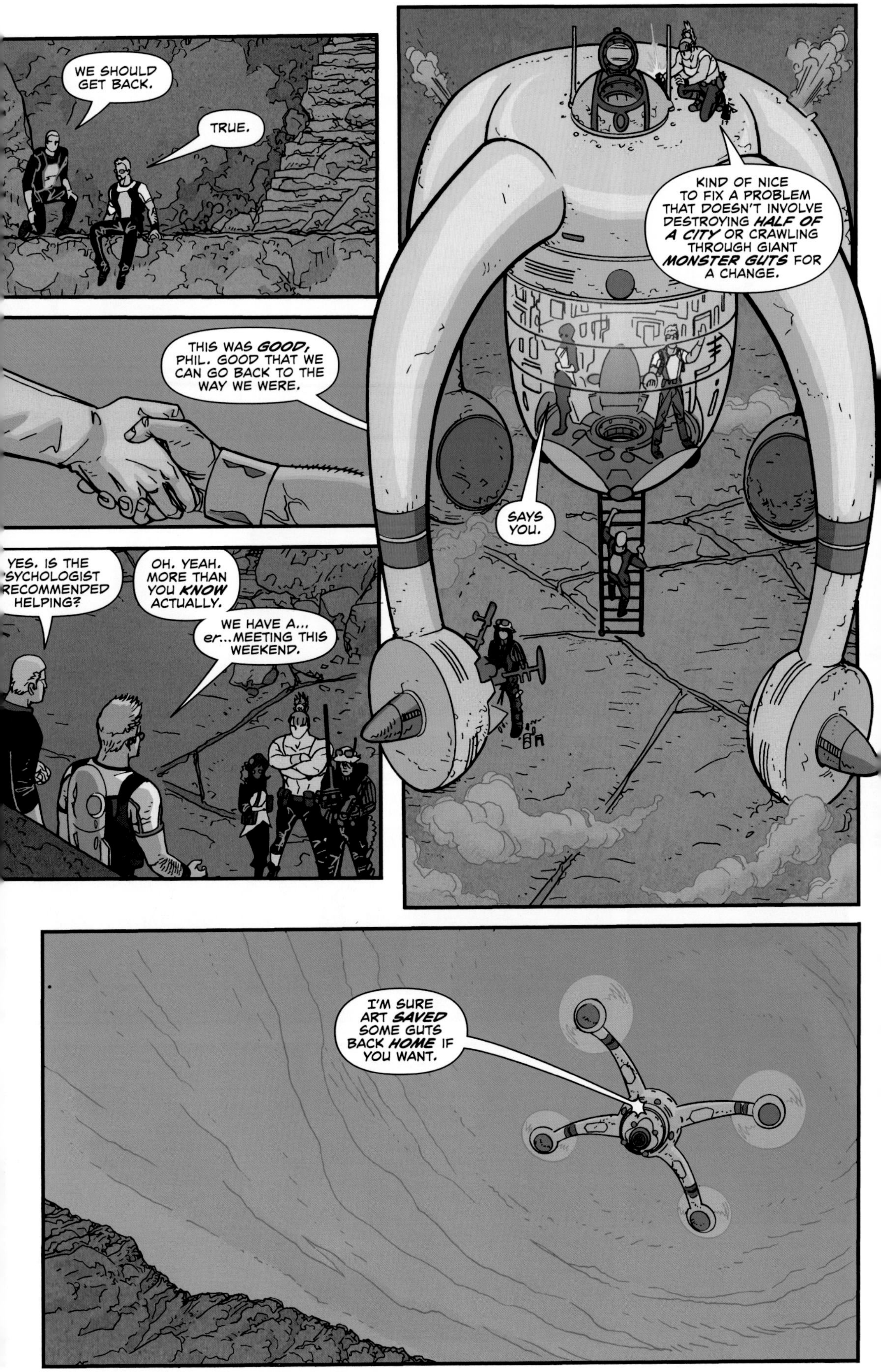

WE SHOULD GET BACK.
TRUE.

THIS WAS **GOOD,** PHIL. GOOD THAT WE CAN GO BACK TO THE WAY WE WERE.

YES. IS THE SYCHOLOGIST RECOMMENDED HELPING?
OH. YEAH. MORE THAN YOU ***KNOW*** ACTUALLY.
WE HAVE A... *er*...MEETING THIS WEEKEND.

KIND OF NICE TO FIX A PROBLEM THAT DOESN'T INVOLVE DESTROYING ***HALF OF A CITY*** OR CRAWLING THROUGH GIANT ***MONSTER GUTS*** FOR A CHANGE.
SAYS YOU.

I'M SURE ART SAVED SOME GUTS BACK HOME IF YOU WANT.

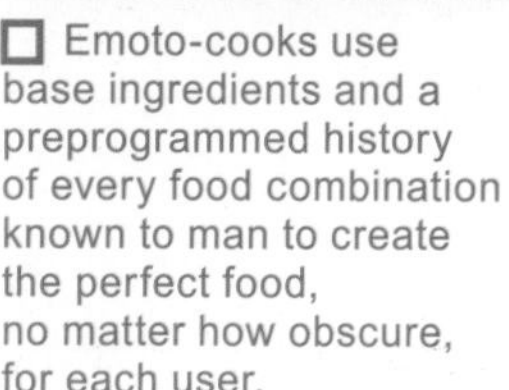

Emoto-cooks use base ingredients and a preprogrammed history of every food combination known to man to create the perfect food, no matter how obscure, for each user.

Cheeseburger: See Herbert June Travelogue report, chapter

Somewhere in New Mexico.
THERE'S SOMETHING I WANT TO *SHOW* YOU.

WE HAVE TO LOCATE, DOCUMENT, AND CONTAIN EVERY TIME TEAR. BUT NOT ALL OF THE TEARS ARE EQUAL.

SOME ARE LARGE AND *MALIGNANT* LIKE CHICAGO.

BUT SOME ARE INFINITESIMAL. LESS A PORTAL, AND MORE A TINY *WINDOW.* TAKE A LOOK...

I'M GUESSING IT'S A HOLE TEN THOUSAND YEARS INTO YOUR FUTURE OR YOUR PAST. IT'S REALLY *IMPOSSIBLE* TO TELL.

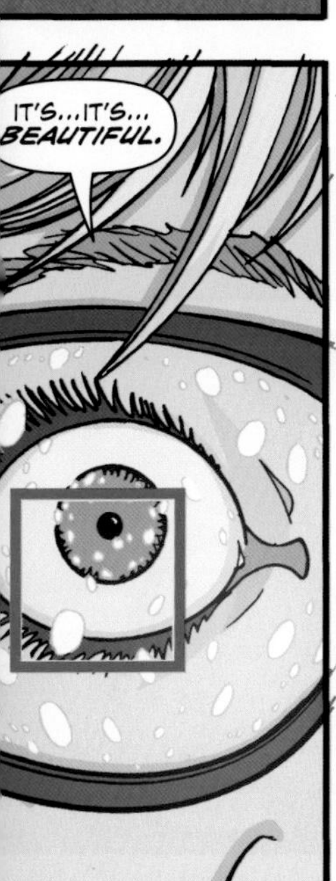

IT'S...IT'S... *BEAUTIFUL.*

IS IT... IS IT *SAFE?*
YEAH. I PUT A MEME-BRANE OVER IT SO WE CAN LOOK IN, BUT NOTHING MICROSCOPIC CAN GET OUT. IT'S REALLY JUST--
ART...

WHAT IS IT, CONNIE?

A naked sense of wonder and love.

☐ The Ultimate Massager is a relaxation device that taps into the user's cerebellum and creates a rhythmic patter of nonsense words and syllables that create a euphoric and—in rare instances—orgasmic state.

HERBERT TRAVELOGUE (excerpt)

December 2014.

As the winter months moved in on us, I decided to embark on a new twenty-first-century experience by visiting a local *club* for a musical performance. After perusing the local newspaper(!), which listed a wide variety of performers ranging from lurid to pedestrian, I settled on a four-piece band called the Pistolwhips.

Once at the venue--a small "concert hall" that was literally the cellar of the restaurant above it--I immediately regretted the outing. The entire venue was carcinogen filled. Scanning the air quality with my optical-lens sensors I picked up large doses of THC, CBC, CBE, CBG, CBT, FKT, and over eight hundred different chemicals that I'd thought had been long lost and/or banned in prehistory.

I fought the urge to hold my breath and, instead, just breathed deeply and normally along with the crowd around me, but only after installing an extra layer of micro superfilters in my ears, nose, and throat.

Surrounded by a muttering, sweaty, and anxious group of concertgoers, I couldn't help but get excited right along with them. Of course, this anticipation and excitement were, in reality, caused by a chemically induced sense of anxiety, but I tried to put that thought out of my head and just let the entire experience wash over me.

After an interminable period of milling about while listening to prerecorded music over the crude (don't get me started) sound system, the lights eventually lowered to increase anticipation (I'm guessing) for the night's entertainment.

◊ ◊ ◊ ◊ ◊ ◊

How can I say this? The next forty minutes were some of the longest minutes of my life. I was immediately hit with a wall of sound--sounds that I would (much later) identify as the musical ejaculate of two crudely handmade *guitars*, a *drum set*, and the singer's voice.

The failings of the sound system were exacerbated by the vocalist's inability to enunciate and his insistence on pressing his mouth directly onto the vocal intake (*microphone*). To make matters worse, the crowd began screaming and pumping their fists to the "beat"--a term I use very loosely here. Several minutes into the first "song," the entire crowd was actually dancing. My unbelieving eyes took this in even as I slipped another several layers of membrane over my eardrums.

As what I can only describe as waves of sound washed over us, the movement of the crowd became even more frenetic. What I first thought were the beginnings of a physical altercation was actually an accepted form of ritual dance. What I ended up witnessing was a small group of malcontents and social misfits, hungry for human interaction and physical contact, who, unable to procure either one of those things through normal (of this time) social interaction, achieve a sense of well-being and acceptance by throwing their bodies at one another.

With no proper--or, I suspect, legal--ventilation, the cellar became an overheated miasma of sweat, testosterone, pheromones, sexual frustration, chemicals (see the aforementioned list), and violence. Caught in the middle, I regretted not packing the exosuit-slim that Marge had suggested. Soon I was pushed, elbowed, and jostled to the front of the pack. By the time I made it to the front of the stage, I found the violence to be not angry, but rather therapeutic.

For a brief moment I stared up at the stage and the lead singer, veins popping from his neck, face red as he screamed at the surging crowd, and I had a moment of clarity. For those few seconds something in me--something long lost, a slim neural connection to a prehistory me--was discovered. What happened after, I am ashamed to admit as a science professional . . . was a blur.

Needless to say, I returned home concussed, covered in chemicals of every known type and origin, with torn clothes, several bruised ribs, and a lacerated lip. I also possessed a laceration on my elbow that I believe was most likely caused by my purposeful contact with another concertgoer's teeth.

Most egregious of all, however, was the damage that no Thera-bot could fix. Inflicted on me was a new knowledge . . . a new, I hesitate to say it, *appreciation* for a crude time and its savage ways.

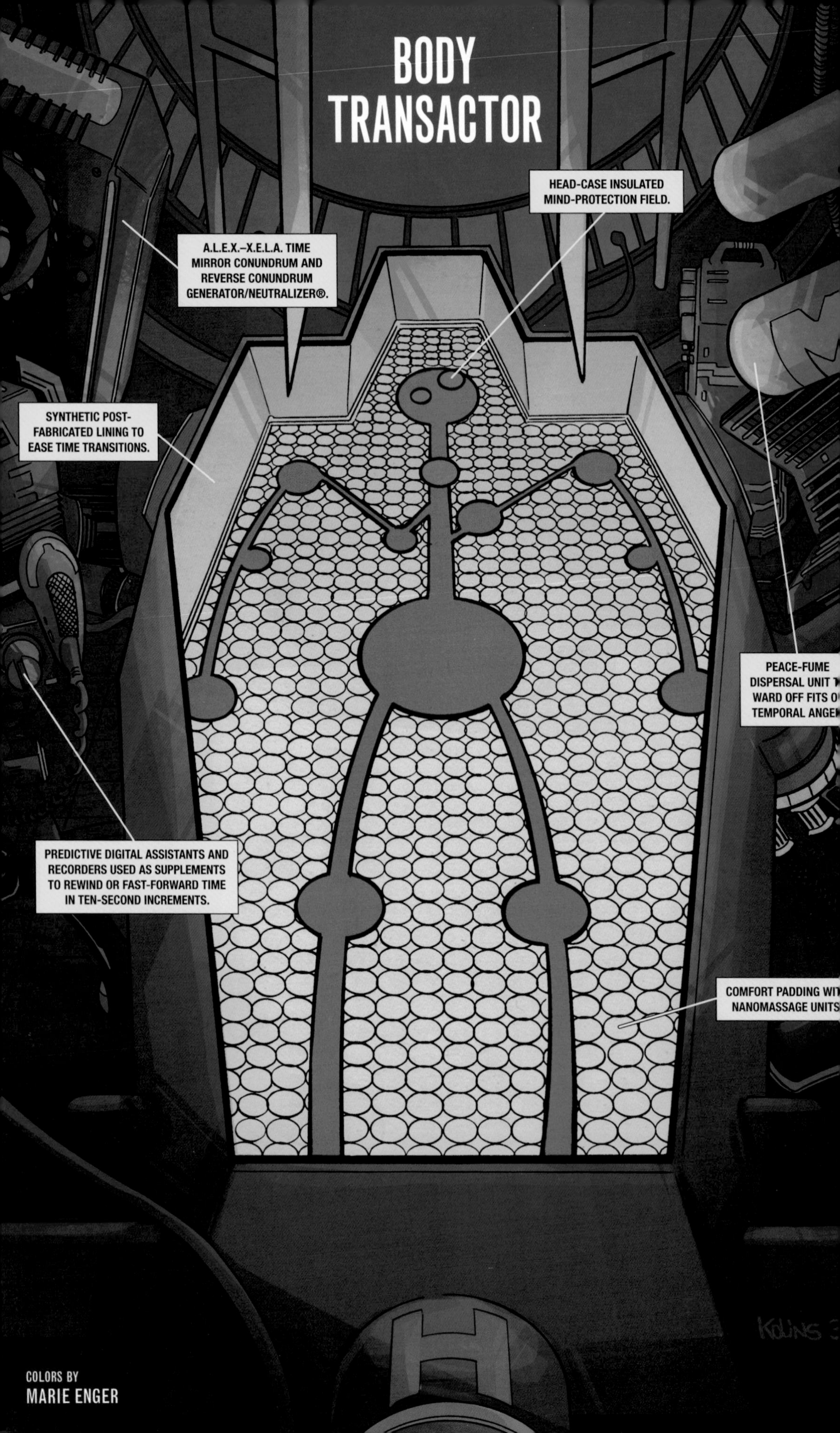
BODY TRANSACTOR
HEAD-CASE INSULATED MIND-PROTECTION FIELD.
A.L.E.X.–X.E.L.A. TIME MIRROR CONUNDRUM AND REVERSE CONUNDRUM GENERATOR/NEUTRALIZER®.
SYNTHETIC POST-FABRICATED LINING TO EASE TIME TRANSITIONS.
PEACE-FUME DISPERSAL UNIT T WARD OFF FITS O TEMPORAL ANGE
PREDICTIVE DIGITAL ASSISTANTS AND RECORDERS USED AS SUPPLEMENTS TO REWIND OR FAST-FORWARD TIME IN TEN-SECOND INCREMENTS.
COMFORT PADDING WI NANOMASSAGE UNITS
KOLINS
COLORS BY
MARIE ENGER

PAST AWAYS™
MATT KINDT SCOTT KOLINS
WES DZIOBA
KOLINS 1984

ROPHY
ROOM
VVVVVVVVVVVVVVV
VVVVVVV
VVVVV
Now.

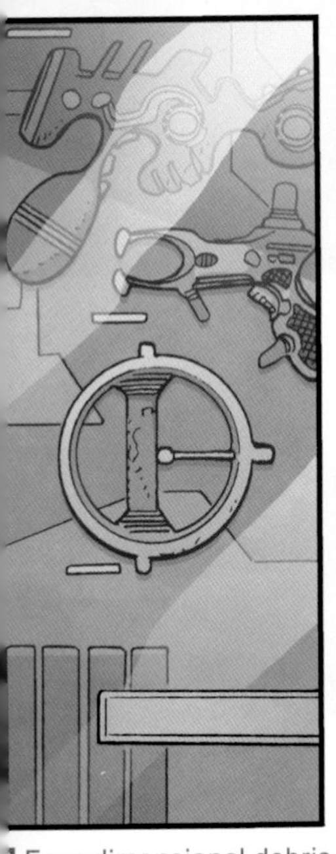

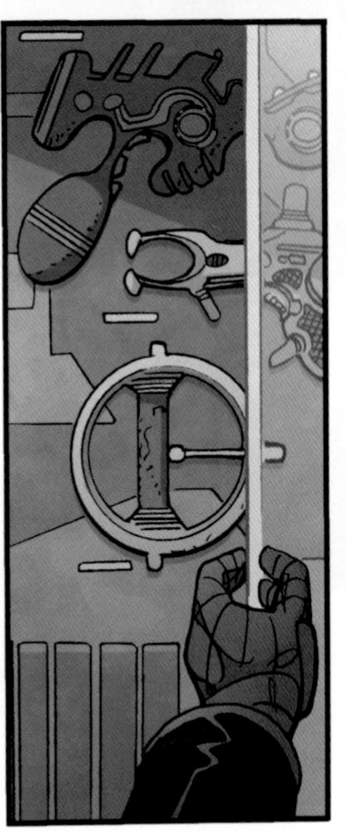

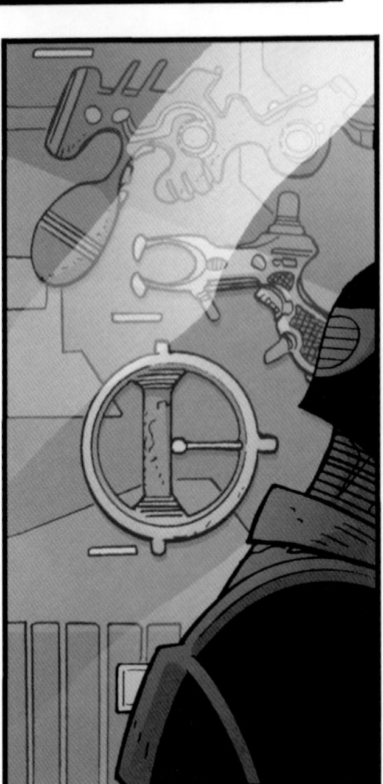

The Sword of the Forgotten Ones, which inflicts wounds that the receiver immediately forgets they've received.

Twenty-first-century grenade launche

One week ago.
JUST GET INTO THE BASE HOWEVER YOU CAN. WITH YOUR TIME SICKNESS, YOU CAN STILL REWIND TIME TWENTY MINUTES, SO IF YOU MAKE A MISTAKE YOU SHOULD BE OKAY.
ONCE YOU GET PAST THE HEADQUARTERS' DEFENSES, JUST WAIT. I'M NOT SURE WHAT KIND OF TRAPS ARTHUR HAS IN PLACE, SO JUST... TAKE IT SLOW.
ONCE YOU'RE INSIDE, WAIT FOR US. IT NEEDS TO BE A SURPRISE. TO ME AS WELL.
JUST KEEP REWINDING TIME UNTIL YOU'VE DONE IT. ARTHUR IS YOUR TARGET. YOU WON'T BE ABLE TO GET ANYONE ELSE. GET HIM AND GET OUT.
Now.
INTRUDER ALERT! STAIRS REQUESTING PERMISSION TO USE LETHAL MODE OF INCAPACITATION.
YOU SURE WE HAVEN'T SEEN THIS MOVIE BEFORE? I FEEL LIKE I'VE SEEN IT.
REQUEST PERMISSION TO USE LETHAL--
IS THAT THE STAIRS TALKING AGAIN?

Neoclassical meta-postmodern film from the twenty-ninth century, *The Gynomorph from the Lagune Noire.*

BOOOOM

I'M GETTING *TIRED* OF FIGHTING ART'S TROPHY-ROOM RELICS.

PLEASE-- WHOEVER YOU ARE! YOU *CAN'T HURT US...* LET'S JUST *TALK* ABOUT WHATEVER'S BOTHERING YOU...

Sigh

KEEP HIM BUSY WHILE I GET A SCAN...

"NOT SURE WHO HE WAS" IS WHAT WE'RE GONNA PUT ON YOUR *GRAVE CAPSULE.*

JUST THOUGHT YOU SHOULD KNOW--

TNG

BOOO
SEE?

DESTINY. WE WEREN'T *MEANT* TO DIE.

BUT I THINK *YOU*--

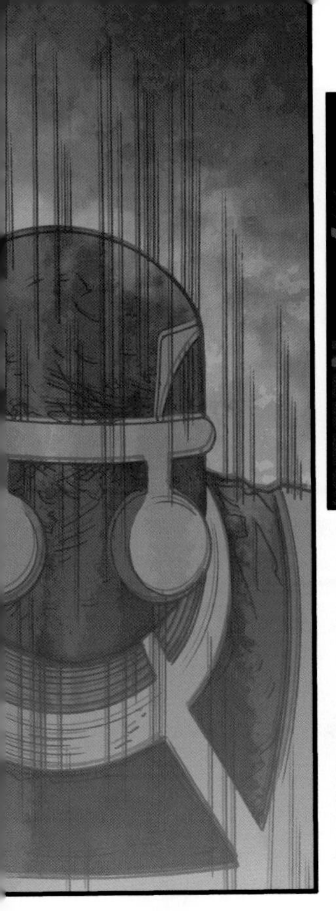

KLIK
KLIK
JUST THOUGHT YOU SHOULD KNOW--

GRAK

SEE?
DESTINY. WE WEREN'T MEANT TO DIE.

JUST THOUGHT YOU SHOULD KNOW--

SEE?

DESTINY. WE WEREN'T MEANT TO DIE.

YOU SURE WE HAVEN'T SEEN THIS MOVIE BEFORE? I FEEL LIKE I'VE SEEN IT.

HEIN! NO-- WAIT!

IT'S POINTLESS RIGHT NOW--YOU'VE GOT TO WAIT UNTIL ARTHUR COMES BACK!
REWIND TIME AND WAIT IT OUT.

OKAY.

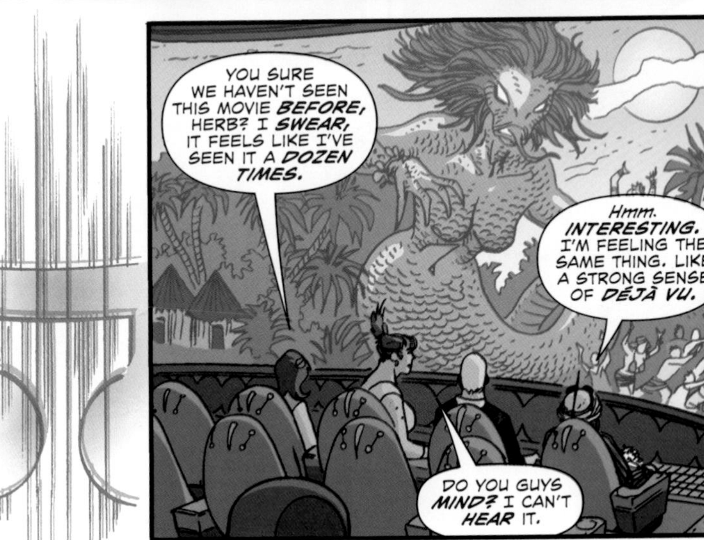
YOU SURE WE HAVEN'T SEEN THIS MOVIE BEFORE, HERB? I SWEAR, IT FEELS LIKE I'VE SEEN IT A DOZEN TIMES.
Hmm. INTERESTING. I'M FEELING THE SAME THING. LIKE A STRONG SENSE OF DÉJÀ VU.
DO YOU GUYS MIND? I CAN'T HEAR IT.

Shoulder-mounted atomizer with an ion blast capable of slicing through 100,000 miles of bedrock.

I HAD A WONDERFUL EVENING, ART.

ME TOO.

I DON'T...I DON'T USUALLY **SEE** MY PATIENTS.
I'M NOT A PATIENT **ANYMORE,** CONNIE.
I KNOW.

I USUALLY DON'T MOVE THIS **FAST.** I'D...I'D INVITE YOU **UP,** BUT I JUST WANT TO TAKE IT **SLOW.**

DON'T WORRY. WE'VE GOT **ALL THE TIME** IN THE WORLD.
I LOOK FORWARD TO IT.
NEXT TIME, ART. NEXT TIME I'LL HAVE YOU UP.

WELCOME HOME, ARTHUR. MAY I TRANSPORT YOU SOMEWHERE?
WHERE'S THE REST OF THE TEAM? TAKE ME THERE.

CERTAINLY. THEY ARE CURRENTLY MAKING REPAIRS TO THE LEVEL SIX BELIEF-SUSPENSION SYSTEMS.

THANK YOU.

WHAT HAPPENED TO THE SUSPENSION SYSTEM?

HEY, ART! NO IDEA.
WE THINK THE TORTOISE CONFLICT LAST MONTH TAXED THE SYSTEM...I NOTICED THE ENTIRE HEADQUARTERS WAS LISTING NEARLY THREE DEGREES...

LESS TALK AND MORE FIXING, PLEASE. THIS THING AIN'T LIGHT.
GOOD TO SEE YOU.

HAVE YOU TRIED FILLING THE PILOT HOLES AND RESETTING THE BACK STORIES?
WE DID, BUT IT'S STILL UNSTABLE.
HOW'S YOUR NEW GIRLFRIEND, ART? ALL GOOD?
Hm? OH, YEAH. CONNIE. SHE'S FANTASTIC. WE'RE TAKING IT SLOW, BUT--

MISSED.

Miniature laser blaster nicknamed the "Coup Maker" for its integral role in the overthrow of the ruthless third Martian mine spider regime.

AND WHO MIGHT *YOU* BE? OBVIOUSLY SOMEONE *NOT FAMILIAR* WITH US.

SWEAR THIS HAS HAPPENED *BEFORE...*
CHOOM

MAYBE I ALREADY PUNCHED THIS GUY INTO *NEXT TUESDAY...?*

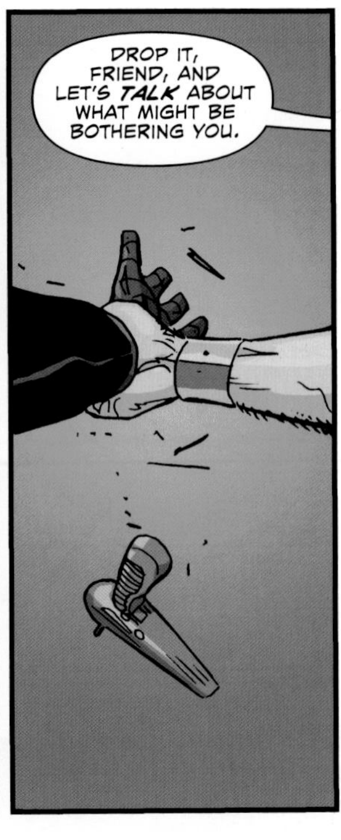
DROP IT, FRIEND, AND LET'S *TALK* ABOUT WHAT MIGHT BE BOTHERING YOU.

HOLD HIM STILL, ART...

BZZAPK
WHAT THE--?!

HOW...
HOW...THIS ISN'T HAPPENING...

GRAHHHHH!

IMPOSSIBLE...!

COME ON! DON'T LET THIS FOOL GET AWAY!

DRIVE HIM TO STAIRS--AND HAVE STAIRS *TELEPORT* HIM BACK HERE. WE'LL BE *READY!*

YOU *HEARD* HIM, STAIRS. SEND US BACK DOWN...!

I'VE BEEN WORKING ON A PORTABLE PORTAL TO THE UNTIMES.

DIDN'T THINK I'D HAVE TO *TES*
IT SO SOON... BUT *HERE GOES.*

I'LL OPEN IT UP...AND THEN WE SHOVE THIS GUY IN.
I'M NOT SURE... WHO *IS* HE? HOW DID HE...HOW DID HE *KILL ART?!* WE AREN'T *ABLE* TO DIE BEFORE WE'RE BORN, PHIL. WE NEED TO *STUDY...*

TAKE US *BACK* TO THE SUSPENSION ROOM! *NOW!*
WITH PLEASURE, MARGARET.

I'VE *GOT* HIM, *MARGE!*

FSZZZSHT

--THE *HELL?*

IT'S A PORTAL TO THE *UNTIMES.* HE WON'T...HE *CAN* HURT US AGAIN...

I THOUGHT...

I THOUGHT WE COULDN'T BE *KILLE* TIME *PROTECTED* U WE CAN'T DIE BEFOR WE WERE BORN...TIM *PROTECTS* ITSELF. PROTECTS US...

AN ASSASSIN SENT FROM OUR TIME? HE MUST HAVE FOUND A *LOOPHOLE.*
IMPOSSIBLE TO KNOW, NOW THAT HE'S *GONE*...

ART...

OH... ART...

IMPOSSIBLE...

Later...

YOU CAN CURE ME, RIGHT? YOU SAID YOU'D FIX ME.

DON'T WORRY. I'LL FIX EVERYTHING.

HERBERT JUNE TRAVELOGUE (excerpt)

January 2015.

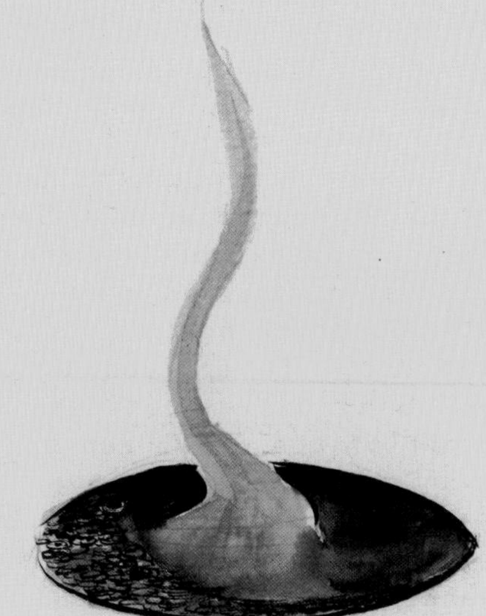

Taking a walk through the crisp January weather, I was once again reminded of how crudely the citizens of the twenty-first century live. With no weather control in place, it is literally a surprise every time I leave the headquarters. There is no official way to predict the weather, let alone bend it into favorable conditions. Very disconcerting.

However, I braced myself for a brisk walk through gusty, ice-cold winds and ducked into a random shop along Main Street. In my experience so far, there are so many new and different stimuli in this world that nearly every random outing is sure to bring a uniquely odd experience.

Today, as I ducked into a hitherto-unknown retail establishment, I was bombarded by music and a smell that I can only describe as . . . intriguing. A smell that was like a unique blend of fresh earth and . . . cat urine.

After walking to the counter, I stood in a queue, awaiting my turn to order. Absent from this retail booth were any traces of psycho-anticipatory devices that would have surely sped up the ordering process. Instead, I had to wait an interminable amount of time before expressing my desire for a product through simple verbal commands to a human who took my order.

Unsure of what to get, I simply repeated the order of the customer ahead of me. After verbally expressing my desired product, I again had to pay with hard currency. An inefficient, but nonetheless charming, ritual, usually followed by an obvious additional payment into a cup as a nonverbal expression of appreciation for service rendered. A "tip," it is called.

My name was asked for and given, and I noticed that it was rather hurriedly and only partly accurately scrawled onto my drinking receptacle. I stepped away from the line and turned to find a seat. As I sat at a small wooden (!) table, I was unsure of the next step. I did not receive the item I ordered. How long was I to wait?

After several minutes of observing the patterns of behavior of those around me, it soon became clear that there was no part of this mysterious service that was automated. The product was being prepared by an all-human task force that, while not happy in the endeavor, seemed not to mind the tasks before them. In fact, they often laughed and found community with each other amid their shared work.

After approximately five minutes, my name was called out. There was no silent mental alert or subcutaneous alarm--and how could there be in this primitive era? I rose and retrieved my product. It arrived in a small paper (!) cup. I took it back to my designated sitting area and sat down. I took the lid off of the small cup and held it to my nose. The familiar cat-urine/earth smell overwhelmed my senses. Looking around at the civilians who also sat drinking from similar cups, I knew that I would have to put this liquid to my lips, whether I wanted to or not. I could not divine the purpose of such a small drink, so inefficiently crafted and so unappealing to the senses. But what is the purpose of an explorer if not to test the unknown . . . to step into the foreign and report their findings?

And so I did. I poured the steaming black liquid over my lips and slowly sipped. It was hot. It was bitter. But I choked it down as best I could. I finished it in one go, not wanting to delay or prolong the experience. I simply wanted it done.

I can honestly say there was no pleasure in the tasting. I wondered at those around me who all seemed full of vigor and joy. How did this bitter liquid bring them together? And keep them in this state?

I rose to leave, and as I walked home, something curious happened. My pulse quickened. It seemed as if my very thoughts were racing faster than my consciousness could keep up. I stared at the world around me with renewed wonder and interest. My mood was lifted. My body felt like it was coursing with an energy the likes of which I hadn't felt since I was a child.

When I returned to headquarters, I immediately went to the lab to analyze my blood and bodily fluids. The substance that I had innocently imbibed was laced with large amounts of caffeine. An immense, concentrated dose. There were no limits set . . . no carefully controlled dispensary drones or microcapsule automated-administration suppositories to deliver this product.

There were no safeguards. No subcutaneous neurosensors to monitor my heart and health as I took in this . . . this . . . most wonderful of controlled substances.

I spent the next seventy-two hours unable to sleep. I was afraid to return to this "coffee shop" and at the same time found myself constantly spinning new excuses and making plans to return every single day that we remain here in the twenty-first century.

The gynomorph from the Lagune noire

Dark Horse Pictures proudly presents

A Matt Kindt–Scott Kolins production
presented in six dimensions®

ART BY
MATT KINDT

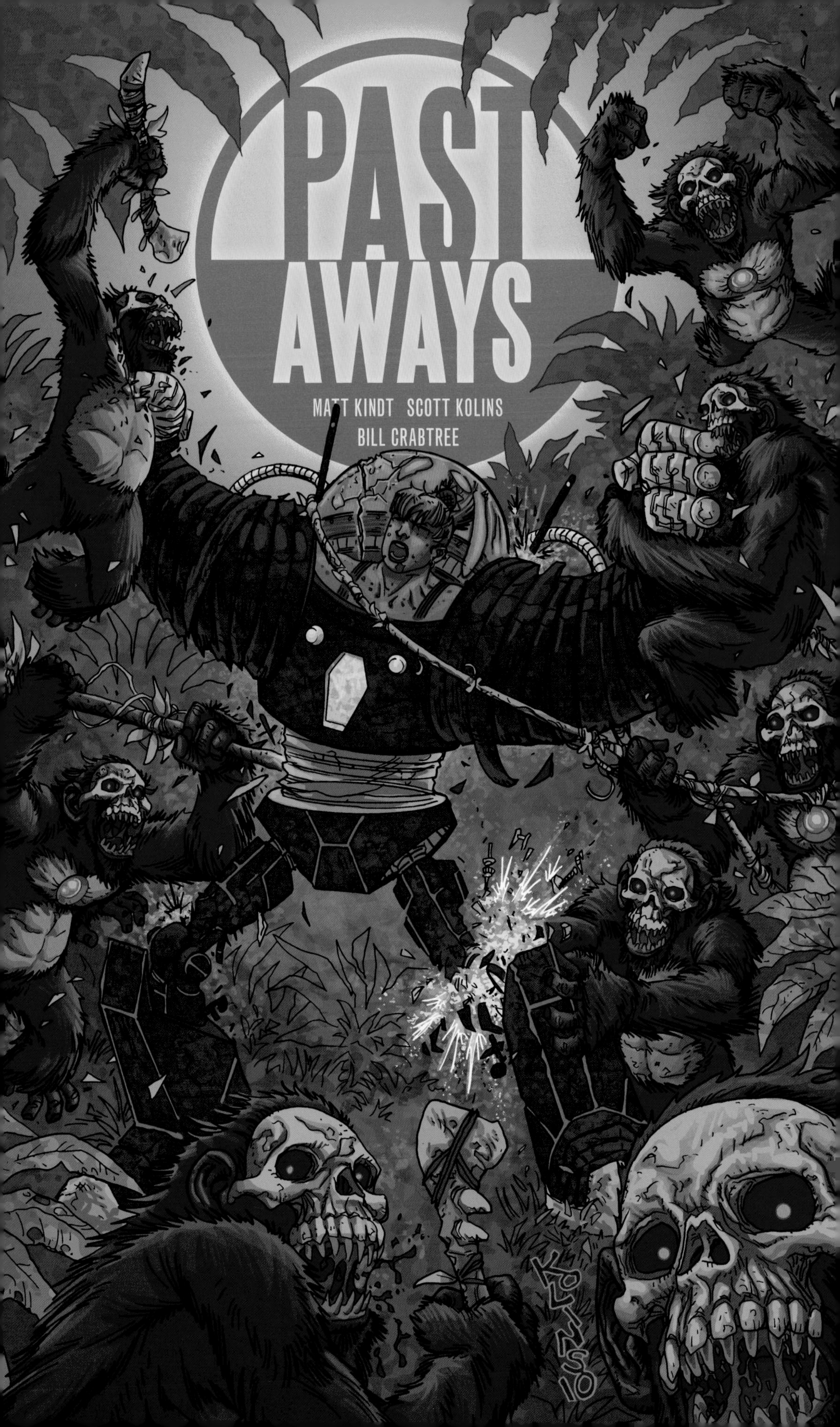
PAST
AWAYS
MATT KINDT SCOTT KOLINS
BILL CRABTREE
KOLINS 10

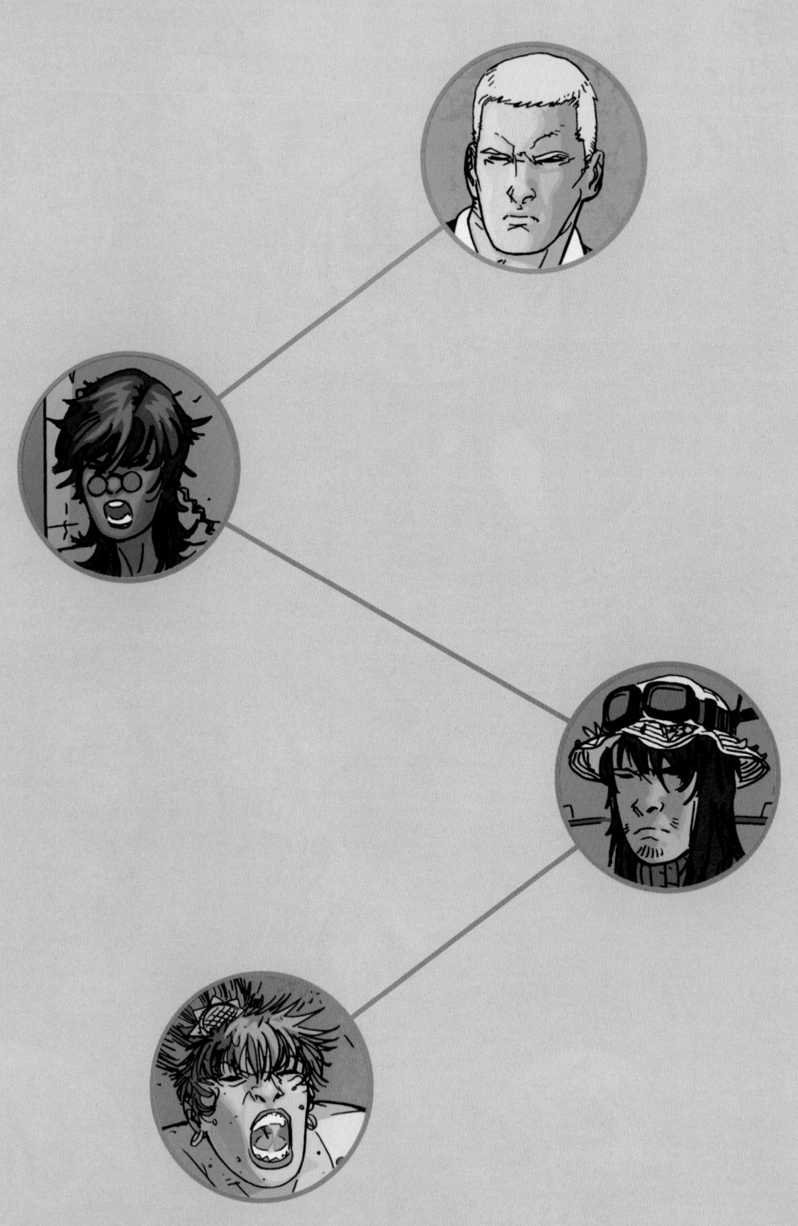

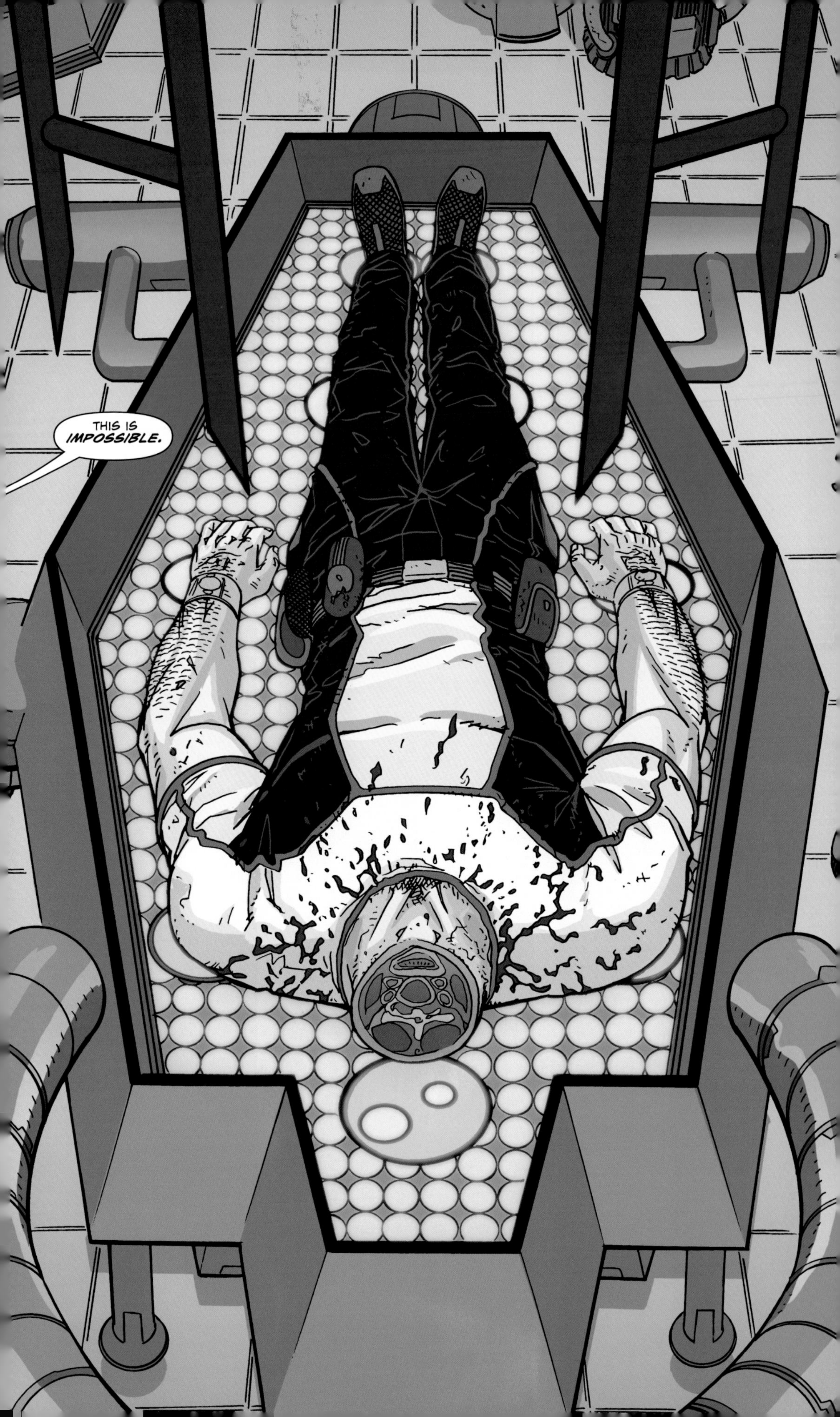

THIS IS *IMPOSSIBLE.*

"TIME PROTECTS ITSELF AT ALL COSTS.

"WE KNOW THIS. IT WON'T ALLOW A CONUNDRUM. THIS IS WHY YOU CAN'T KILL YOUR OWN GREAT-GREAT-GRANDFATHER.

"THIS IS WHY WE HAVE BEEN UNABLE TO DIE SINCE WE LANDED IN THE PAST.

"TIME...FATE... WHATEVER YOU WANT TO CALL IT...KEEPS US ALIVE BECAUSE WE CANNOT DIE BEFORE WE WERE BORN.

"BUT OUR LEADER...ART LIES BEFORE US...DEAD. HOW DID THIS HAPPEN? HOW COULD THIS HAPPEN?

"I HAVE A THEORY... A THEORY I'VE BEEN WORKING ON FOR QUITE SOME TIME THAT I CALL THE TIME TRUMP.

"TIME WILL DO WHATEVER IT TAKES TO PROTECT ITSELF FROM CONUNDRUMS. AND IN OUR CASE...THAT HAS MEANT PRESERVING OUR LIVES.

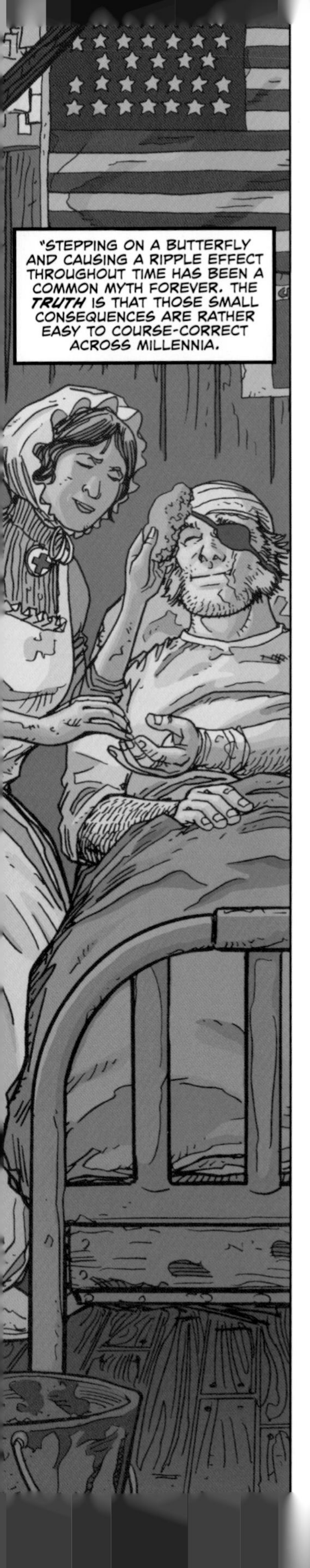
"STEPPING ON A BUTTERFLY AND CAUSING A RIPPLE EFFECT THROUGHOUT TIME HAS BEEN A COMMON MYTH FOREVER. THE TRUTH IS THAT THOSE SMALL CONSEQUENCES ARE RATHER EASY TO COURSE-CORRECT ACROSS MILLENNIA.

"WHAT WOULD BE LESS EASY TO CORRECT IS A NARRATIVE IN WHICH A FAMILY TREE IS DISRUPTED...WITH EITHER AN UNNATURAL DEATH OR... A ROMANCE THAT SHOULD HAVE NEVER BEEN.

"MY HEREDITARY SUPERSCANS HAVE GIVEN ME THE ANSWER. ARTHUR WAS A MAN OUT OF TIME, AND TIME PROTECTED HIM TO AVOID HIS DEATH BEFORE HE WAS BORN. HOWEVER...ARTHUR FLIPPED TIME'S TRUMP CARD WHEN HE ENGAGED IN A ROMANCE WITH CONNIE... THE PSYCHIATRIST THAT PHIL RECOMMENDED.

"ARTHUR'S RELATIONSHIP WITH CONNIE WAS NEVER MEANT TO BE. CONNIE IS A DISTANT RELATIVE OF ART'S, AND SO THEIR UNION COULD NEVER...AND ***SHOULD*** NEVER HAVE BEEN. TO PREVENT THIS HAPPENING, TIME PLAYED ITS TRUMP CARD.

"THEIR RELATIONSHIP WOULD HAVE ***IRREVOCABLY*** CHANGED THE TIMELINE OF THE FUTURE...SENDING RIPPLE EFFECTS THROUGH THE AGES THAT WOULD BE AN ***EVEN GREATER*** DISRUPTION THAN ART'S OWN DEATH.

"THEREFORE, ARTHUR HAD TO ***DIE*** TO PROTECT THE TIMELINE."
AGAIN

☐ DNA repository designed to collect and archive genetic material.

...TREAD
CAREFULLY...

IT WAS *YOU*, PHIL. YOU *KILLED* ART.

OF COURSE, THE MOST *DULL WITTED* OF YOU WOULD FIGURE IT OUT FIRST. LIKE A *DUMB ANIMAL* ON THE *SCENT*.

I NEVER LIKED YOU, PHIL...

...GLAD TO FINALLY HAVE AN *EXCUSE* TO TEAR YOU AND YOUR FRIEND APART.

I KNOW YOUR *TRICKS.* YOU REWIND TIME UNTIL YOU GET IT RIGHT...

YOU PROCESS YOUR MISTAKE, *ADAPT,* AND REACT DIFFERENTLY.
THE *PROBLEM* YOU'RE GOING TO HAVE...
...IS WHEN I FINALLY *GET IN CLOSE...*
KRASH
...WHAT *HAPPENS* WHEN I GET TO YOU--

--**BEFORE**
OU REALIZE
OU MADE A
MISTAKE?

GYAHHHH!

nNGhh... shuff... I...ALWAYS **KNEW...**

...YOU WERE A SOULLESS... GODLESS... **THING.**

I CAN'T HELP BUT FEEL ***RESPONSIBLE...***

IF WE HADN'T COME BACK HERE...IF I'D ONLY ***PREDICTED*** THE RESULTS. I'M SURPRISED ***PHIL*** DIDN'T SEE THIS COMING...UNLESS... UNLESS PHIL--?

HERB. IT WAS ***YOU.***

IT WAS YOU THAT DID THIS.

WHAT? I'D ***NEVER*** HURT ARTHUR!

NO. NOT ARTHUR. THIS... ***ALL*** OF THIS... I REMEMBER...

☐ Electrolyte dispersal device.

"BACK A YEAR AGO. WHEN WE FIRST GOT STRANDED. AND THE TEAM BROKE UP. I WENT WITH YOU TO NEW YORK.
DOUBLE FEATURE
MARTIAN TIME SLI
VAL KILMER BRIGITTE
DOOR INTO SUMME
MEGAN FOX MORGAN
"TO SUPPORT YOU. SO YOU COULD KEEP WRITING YOUR TRAVELOGUES. I FIGURED, OF ALL OF US, YOU'D BE THE MOST *EMOTIONALLY FRAGILE.*
HOT DOGS $1.25 100% BEEF
HOT DOGS
COLD SODA
BOTTLE WATER
PRETZEL
FRESH HOT PRETZEL
"YOU DIDN'T DO AS MUCH TRAINING AS WE DID. YOU WERE THE JOURNALIST. THE *'EVERYMAN'* SENT ALONG TO PAINT A PICTURE OF THE PAST FOR OUR PRESENT.
"BUT IT WAS THE OPPOSITE. YOU THRIVED. IT WAS LIKE YOU WERE LIVING THIS DREAM.

☐ Mechanically separated turkey, pork, water, corn syrup, beef, salt, paprika extract, etc.

BRYANT PARK
"YOU WERE HAPPY THAT OUR ONE-WEEK JOURNEY HAD TURNED INTO A YEAR WITH NO END IN SIGHT.
"YOU WERE HAPPY TO BE STRANDED. HAPPY TO BE AWAY FROM OUR TIME. OUR LIVES. OUR REALITY.
"LIKE YOU WERE RUNNING FROM SOMETHING AND YOU FINALLY GOT AWAY.
"THAT'S WHAT SENT ME SPIRALING INTO DEPRESSION, HERB. YOU...YOU BEING COMPLETELY CONTENT. NOT NEEDING ME OR ANYONE ELSE."

YOU KNOW MORE THAN YOU'RE TELLING.
...URSULA... WAIT...
WHERE DID MARGE AND PHIL GO?
YOU'RE NOT GOING TO SQUIRM OUT OF THIS ONE, HERB.
WHAT DID YOU DO?! WHAT DO YOU KNOW?!
GET OFF OF ME!

YOU'RE JUST THE TEAM WHORE, YOU KNOW THAT?

YOU'RE KIDDING, RIGHT? I'M THE PSYCHE SPECIALIST. IT'S MY JOB TO KEEP THIS TEAM HARMONIOUS AND HAPPY. I WENT THROUGH YEARS OF TRAINING TO LEARN HOW PEOPLE WORK. TO UNDERSTAND SMALL-TEAM DYNAMICS. TO KEEP EVERYONE IN HARMONY. IT'S A SCIENCE YOU WOULDN'T UNDERSTAND.

WELL, IT LOOKS LIKE YOU'RE DOING A WONDERFUL JOB.

I GET IT NOW.

I REMEMBER... I REMEMBER YOU... THE DAY OF THE MISSION LAUNCH... IT ALL MAKES SENSE!

"WE'D BEEN THROUGH ALL THE TESTS AND TRAINING, BUT SOMETHING *WASN'T WORKING.*
"MISSION CONTROL COULDN'T FIGURE IT OUT.
"WE ALL WANTED TO GO *SO BADLY...*"
...THERE'S A FATAL *FLAW* SOMEWHERE, HERB. IF WE DON'T PASS THE TEST LAUNCH TOMORROW, THEY'RE *SCRAPPING* THE ENTIRE PROGRAM. NO ONE'S BEEN ABLE TO FIGURE IT OUT. IF WE DON'T LAUNCH...IT JUST *WASN'T MEANT TO BE.* I'M SORRY.

Parasitic control device used for noncorporeal entities as a way of integrating with the physical world.

"WE ALL WANTED TO GO SO BADLY...
"BUT YOU MOST OF ALL."
SO THAT'S IT?
LOOKS LIKE IT. WE GET ONE MORE TEST TOMORROW.

Various works-in-progress device. All currently nonfunctioning.

"I KNOW YOUR BACKSTORY, HERB. IT WAS MY JOB.
"YOU LOST YOUR FAMILY IN THE SECOND DIVINE INVASION.
"YOU HAD NOTHING TO LOSE.
"EXCEPT THE MISSION.
"I KEPT MY EYE ON YOU. I THOUGHT...OF THE ENTIRE TEAM...YOU WERE THE MOST UNSTABLE. THE ONE THAT NEEDED WATCHING.
"I DIDN'T REALIZE WHAT YOU'D DONE AT THE TIME. BUT I KNEW YOU WEREN'T SUICIDAL. SO I DIDN'T THINK TOO MUCH OF IT.

"THE NEXT DAY...IT WAS THE FINAL TRIAL RUN. IF WE DIDN'T PASS, THE ENTIRE PROJECT WAS GOING TO BE SHUT DOWN."

...READINGS ARE STILL TOO UNSTABLE. I'M SORRY, TEAM...BUT WE'RE GOING TO HAVE TO SCRAP THE LAUNCH ***INDEFINITELY.***

"I NEVER PUT IT TOGETHER. JUST THOSE LITTLE THINGS. THINGS YOU ***NOTICE*** AND THEN ***FORGET...***"

...BRACE FOR ANOMALY! SHIP IS LAUNCHING OUTSIDE OF OUR ***CONTROL!***

"SMALL THINGS THAT GET LOST IN THE WRECKAGE OF LARGER EVENTS."

YOU LAUNCHED THE MISSION REMOTELY. WHEN IT WASN'T READY.

YOU SENT US BACK. YOU STRANDED US. AND WHETHER YOU LIKE IT OR NOT, YOU ARE RESPONSIBLE FOR ART.

I CAN FIX THIS. I KNOW WHAT TO DO. I KNOW HOW TO GET US HOME. I ALWAYS DID. AND SO DID ART.

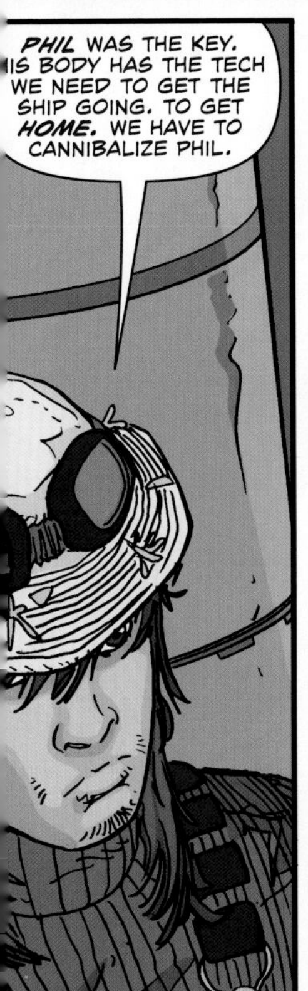
PHIL WAS THE KEY. IS BODY HAS THE TECH WE NEED TO GET THE SHIP GOING. TO GET HOME. WE HAVE TO CANNIBALIZE PHIL.

THEN LET'S GET PHIL.

WHERE'D THEY GO? WHERE'S MARGE?

"WE NEED HER HELP IF WE'RE GOING TO HAVE ANY CHANCE OF TAKING ON PHIL.
"PHIL'S BODY IS THE KEY. IT'S FULL OF THE DELICATE MICROTECH WE'RE GOING TO NEED IF WE EVER WANT TO GET HOME.
"WE NEED TO PRESERVE HIS BODY BEFORE ANYTHING DAMAGES HIM."
The Ultra-Snowflake device. A quantum-level chip designed to instill a sense of self and feelings of individuality. No two chips are exactly alike.

HERBERT JUNE TRAVELOGUE (excerpt)

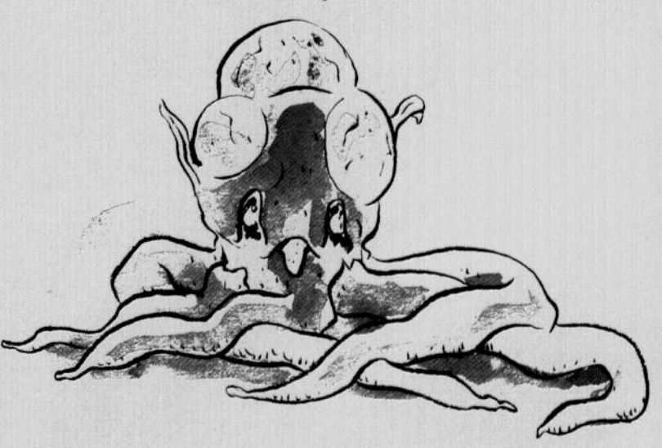

October 2015.

I'm still adjusting to the random and shifting nature of weather here in the twenty-first century. It's a rather odd feeling to wake up every morning and have something so simply controlled as temperature and precipitation be left to chance. But there is also something charming about early humanity's willingness to embrace and adapt to the unknown.

I state all this as preamble to my latest "fall" excursion and participation in the fascinating pagan ritual of donning a crude and rather gaudy (in most cases) ensemble and participating in various local amusements that vary from traditional parties to the lesser-known custom of arriving at randomly selected domiciles, wearing the accoutrements of the holiday, and insinuating that a vague fraud will be committed if a reward is not produced.

Observing this ritual from afar only made me wish to participate in full. I find it my duty as both a scientist and an adventurer of sorts to embed myself as deeply and fully into this strange time as I possibly can, if only to further our understanding of the rudimentary civilization of our ancestors.

With this in mind, I thoroughly ransacked Arthur's trophy room in search of an appropriate costume with which to adorn myself. Suitably dressed, I proceeded to a local *suburb* to subtly embed myself. Having no connection or ability to gain admittance to one of the traditional parties, I availed myself of the more traditional door-to-door activity.

After loitering in the shadows to observe and confirm the proper procedure, I moved forward. I was, admittedly, slightly nervous. Our goal in this time period is to help when we can, but not to influence events or alter the past in any way.

As the last pack of wild roaming costumed youths wandered to the next domicile, I made my move. I tried to remain confident and nonchalant. I was certain that my costume would effectively mask my true identity and also allow me to blend with the general population on this hallowed night.

I rapped gently on the front door and it swung open. Inside I saw two standard adults with expectant smiles on their faces. As quickly as their smiles and greetings appeared, I saw them fade away into looks of horror. The adult male (of what I assume was the traditional male-female family pairing unique to this era) began to turn a bright crimson. His hands reached for his throat and his wife looked at me, eyes wide with horror, and then attended to her collapsing husband.

The man was gasping for air and I stood there dumbfounded, I'm ashamed to say. I hadn't been able to even utter the hallowed greeting before the door was manually slammed shut, effectively sealing me off from the shocking scene.

It was only a matter of a few seconds before I realized the enormity of my mistake. I had unthinkingly chosen several items from Arthur's trophy room to assemble my costume. One of the "items" I was wearing was actually a living specimen we recovered through one of the smaller portal breaches into this time. I was able to identify it as a very early version of what we commonly know as an *Octopus seniorem*--the multibrained, forked-personality creature from billions of years before Earth even existed.

We take the modern *Octopus seniorem* for granted now. Its cranial secretions can be found in nearly every inorganic food we consume in our modern times. But here, humanity had yet to be exposed to these wonders and there was no doubt that the man at the door had suffered an acute allergic reaction to the *Octopus seniorem* that I was wearing on my head as a "mask."

As I said, immediately realizing my mistake, I sealed the *Octopus seniorem* in an atom bag. Then I proceeded to dissolve their (authentic wood!) front door with a semicaustic solvent mist and administered life-saving aid (via AI-driven stents) into the dying man.

Needless to say, I made more of an impact on the twenty-first-century couple than I had intended and immediately removed myself to the hermetic safety of our headquarters. I sit alone now writing this account. I consider this foray to be one of utter failure--never having gotten to utter the magical words of this era's pagan festivity . . . "trick or treat."

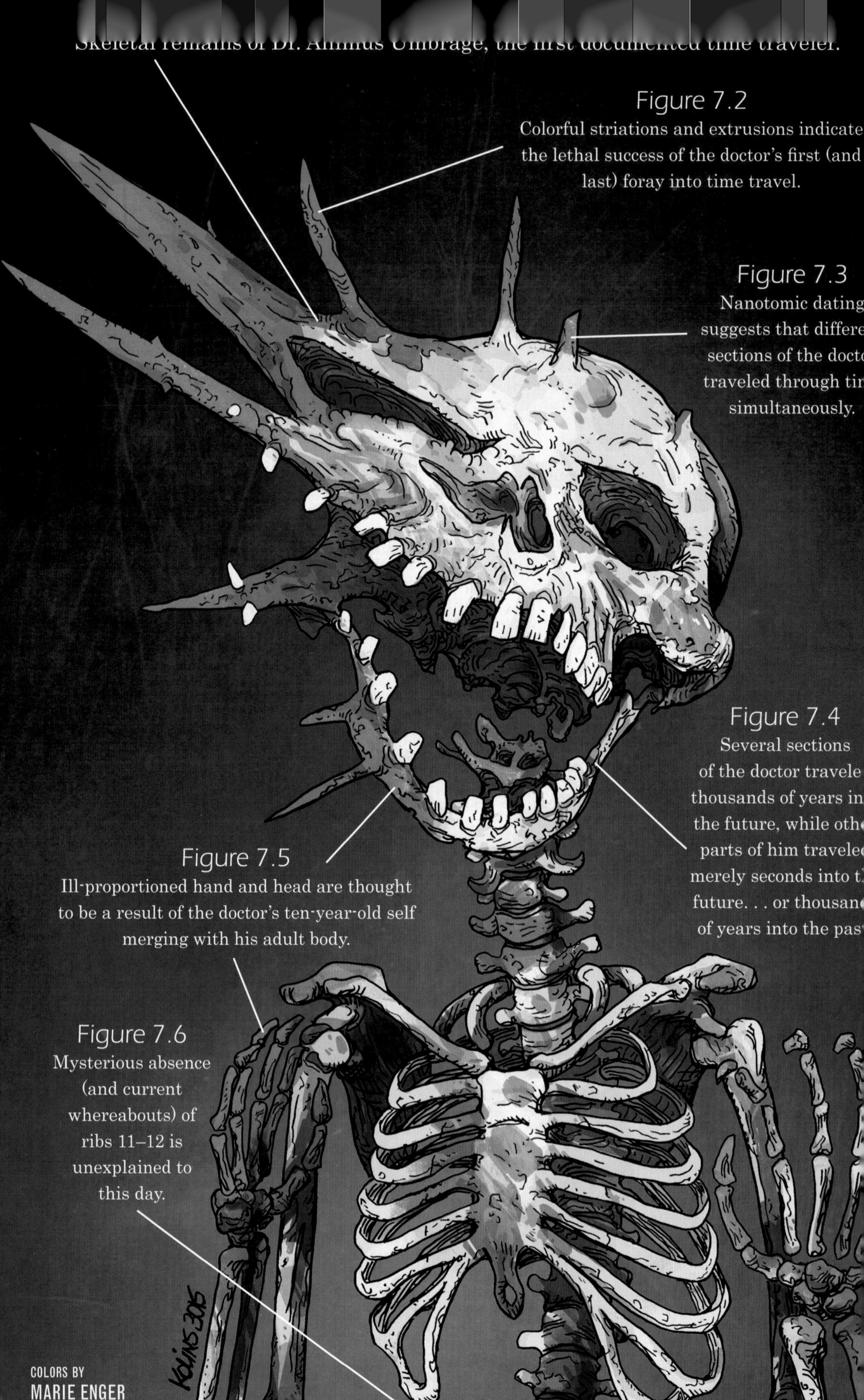

Figure 7.2
Colorful striations and extrusions indicate the lethal success of the doctor's first (and last) foray into time travel.
Figure 7.3
Nanotomic dating suggests that differe sections of the docto traveled through ti simultaneously.
Figure 7.4
Several sections of the doctor travele thousands of years in the future, while oth parts of him travele merely seconds into t future. . . or thousan of years into the pas
Figure 7.5
Ill-proportioned hand and head are thought to be a result of the doctor's ten-year-old self merging with his adult body.
Figure 7.6
Mysterious absence (and current whereabouts) of ribs 11–12 is unexplained to this day.
KOLINS 3015
COLORS BY
MARIE ENGER

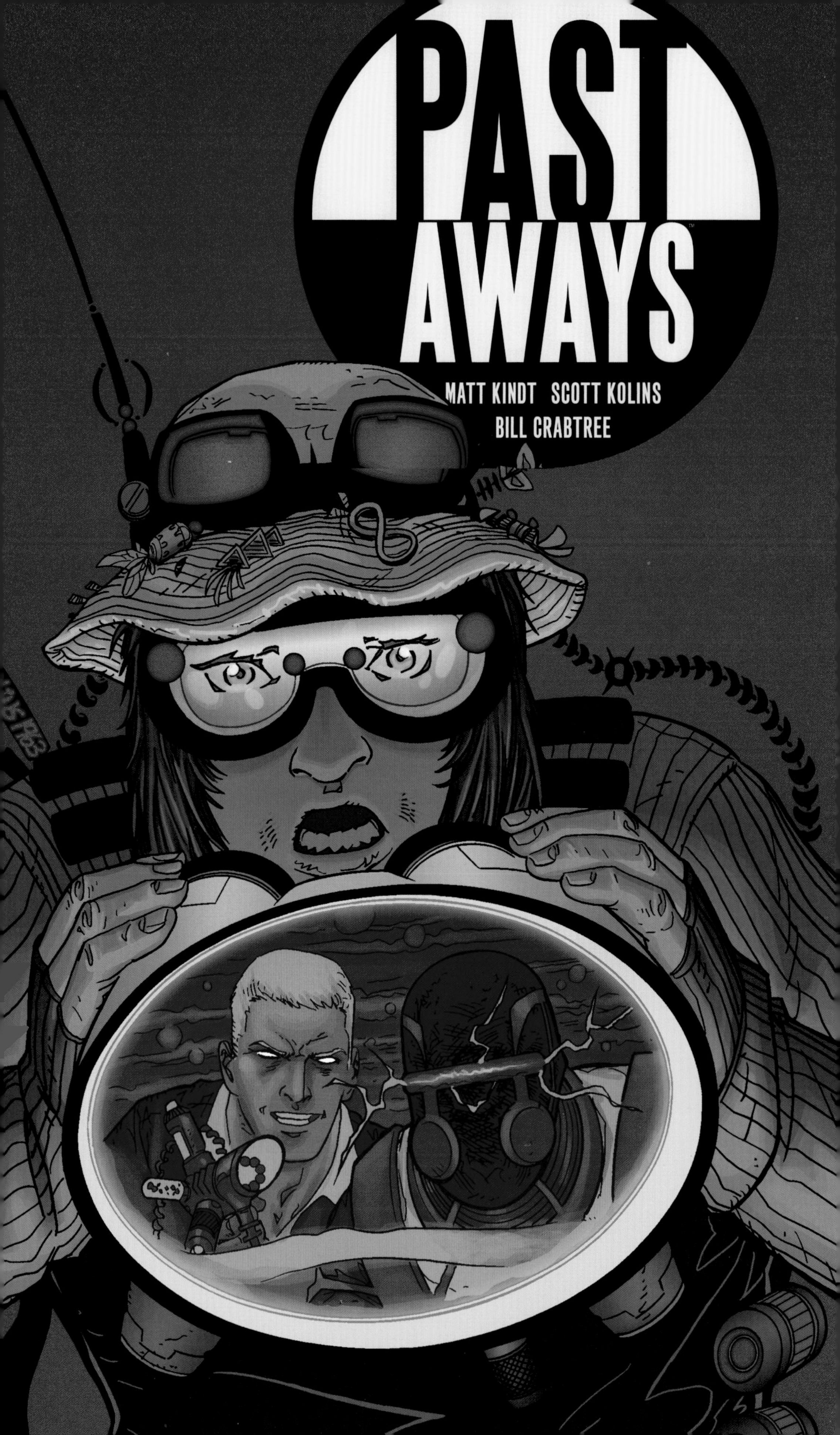
PAST AWAYS
MATT KINDT SCOTT KOLINS
BILL CRABTREE

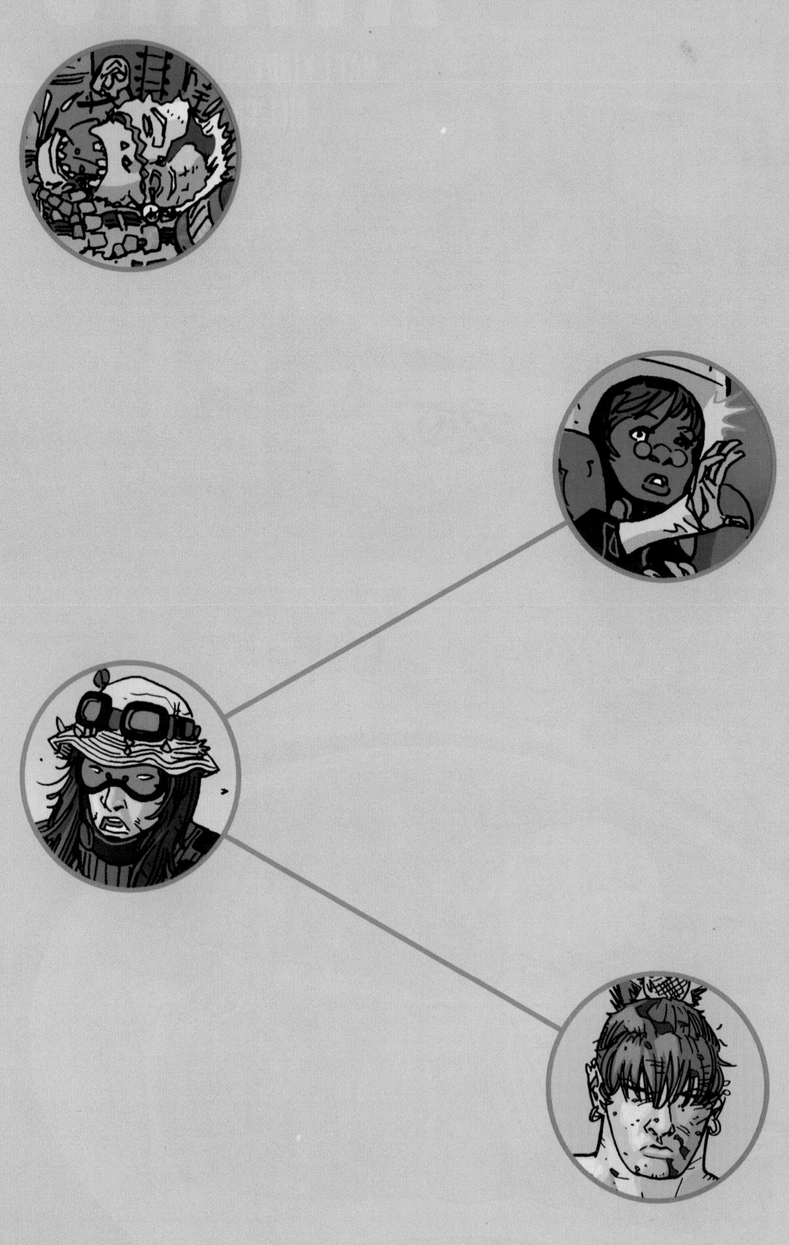

THIS IS ALL ON *YOU*, HERB! YOU SENT US BACK IN TIME! WE'RE *STRANDED* BECAUSE THE TECH WASN'T READY. AND *YOU* SENT US ANYWAY!

ART IS *DEAD* BECAUSE OF YOU!
I WON'T TAKE THAT BLAME! SOME *OTHER AGENT* IS AT WORK HERE. DON'T YOU *SEE?* SOMEONE IS SABOTAGING US! AND WE *CAN* GET HOME. BUT WE'LL HAVE TO CANNIBALIZE PHIL TO DO IT. ARE YOU *PREPARED* FOR THAT?!

WHERE CAN I TAKE YOU?
TAKE ME TO URSULA AND HERB.

☐ Sentient staircase discontinued in year 4300 when the AI Bill of Rights was drafted.

WELL, IF YOU TWO ARE DONE *BICKERING...*

I PUNCHED OUR TICKET HOME.
IT WAS PHIL. HE WAS PARANOID. HE WAS SURE WE WERE GOING TO EVENTUALLY TURN ON HIM. HE WAS SURE WE'D TAKE HIM APART AND USE HIS BRAIN AND BODY TO GET OURSELVES HOME.
SHCHMPFF
WHAT HAPPENED?!
PHIL WAS STOCKING A WAREHOUSE WITH STUFF TO FIGHT US. HE WAS RESPONSIBLE FOR KILLING ART. HE SET IT ALL UP. SENT THAT ASSASSIN. SO I TOOK CARE OF PHIL...
"...AND TOOK CARE OF HIS ASSASSIN."
SO HERE HE IS, HERB.

IF YOU WANT TO GET HOME, NOW YOU'VE GOT THE RAW MATERIAL.

MARGE. HERB IS THE ONE RESPONSIBLE FOR US LAUNCHING ON THIS TRIP. HE'S THE REASON WE'RE STUCK HERE. IF IT WASN'T FOR HIM, NONE OF THIS WOULD HAVE HAPPENED.

WHAT'S SHE SAYING, HERB?

I THOUGHT... I THOUGHT IT WOULD BE SAFE...I WAS SURE I COULD GET US BACK IF ANYTHING WENT WRONG... I JUST...

I WAS DESPERATE. DESPERATE TO LEAVE. TO GO SOMEWHERE. ANYWHERE.
SOMEWHERE BEFORE... BEFORE EVERYTHING FELL APART...
"I'D BEEN OBSESSED WITH TIME TRAVEL SINCE I WAS A KID. THE TANTALIZING ALLURE OF HISTORY BOTH KNOWN AND UNKNOWN...
"I HAD WORKED MY WHOLE LIFE. AMASSING KNOWLEDGE. LEARNING THE SCIENCE. TESTING THEORIES...
"I WAS GOING TO SEE AND HEAR AND TASTE THE PAST IF IT WAS THE LAST THING I DID.
"EVEN IF I DIDN'T HAVE THE BUDGET OR RESOURCES...

"I WENT TOO FAR. MY TUNNEL VISION... MY AMBITION...
"...MADE ME LOSE SIGHT OF WHAT WAS MOST IMPORTANT.
"I HAD GRAND VISIONS FOR MY FAMILY. LIVING IN A PURE, UNTOUCHED HISTORY. WILDERNESS AND SURVIVAL. FREE OF THE DISTRACTIONS OF THE MODERN WORLD.

"I WAS SO *BLINDED* BY THE GOAL...

"...THAT I FAILED TO SEE THE *RISK*.

"*I* WAS CERTAINLY PREPARED TO SACRIFICE ANYTHING AND TO TAKE ANY RISK...

"BUT THE ONE PART OF THE EQUATION I *FAILED* TO RECONCILE...

"...THE MOST *IMPORTANT* PART OF THE EQUATION...

"...WAS THE ONE THAT *RUINED* ME.

CAN'T
AKE NE
THE NE W'Z
YSTERY EXPLOSION
SUBURBS KILLS
ENTIRE FAMILY
"AFTER THAT, I WANTED TO BE ANYWHERE ELSE.
"I DIDN'T CARE ABOUT HISTORY ANYMORE. I SIMPLY WANTED TO BE IN A TIME WHERE I DIDN'T EXIST YET. WHERE I HAVEN'T HAPPENED YET."
WHERE WHAT I'D DONE...
...HASN'T HAPPENED.
HERB. YOU KNOW AS WELL AS I DO THAT YOU CAN'T CHANGE WHAT HAPPENED. BUT YOU CAN CHANGE WHAT'S GOING TO HAPPEN.
WE HAVE PHIL. USE HIM. AND GET US HOME. YOU CAN'T KEEP RUNNING FROM YOUR PAST.

■ Static collar designed to defeat facial recognition and DNA air-sampling police.

THE AI TECH I CANNIBALIZED FROM PHIL'S BRAIN SHOULD HAVE ENOUGH COMPUTING POWER TO CALCULATE A PATH BACK TO OUR TIME.
I'VE HAD THIS WORKED OUT FROM THE BEGINNING. JUST IN CASE PHIL VOLUNTEERED...OR SOMETHING LIKE THIS HAPPENED.
UNFORTUNATELY-- AND PHIL WAS PAINFULLY AWARE OF THIS--IT WILL CUT OUT WHATEVER HUMANITY PHIL HAD IN HIS GRAY MICROMATTER.
WE'RE UNDERPOWERED, SO IT'S GOING TO TAKE SEVERAL JUMPS TO GET US ALL THE WAY BACK. THERE'S ENOUGH JUICE IN MY PACK TO POWER IT, BUT YOU MUST KEEP YOUR CABLES CONNECTED TO MINE. EACH PACK IS ESSENTIAL.
WE EITHER ALL MAKE IT...
ZZZZUUUB
OR NONE OF US DO.
ZZZZZZ ZUUUU IBBB
PIIIWF

FZT

AZZRAK...
PFFSHURPP...
caff...cofff...
KKKRKKK!

43R8
UR5U74
M4RG3
MU57
DI3!!!

WHIREEE
EEEEEEEEEE
EEEEEEEEE!

EEEEEEEEEEEEEEEEEEEE
EEEEEEEEEEEEEEEEEEEEEEEEE
EEEEEEEEEEEEEEEE
EEEEEEEEEEEEEEEE
EEEEEEEEEE
EEEEEEEEEE
KRISHHH
A "Young One" specimen of other-dimensional complex plant life that responds to high-frequency communication.

Unh...
NEED TO CALCULATE OUR *LANDING ERA* SO I CAN PROGRAM THE NEXT *JUMP POINT...*GIVE ME JUST A SECOND...

HERB--!

JUST A MINUTE. I NEED TO FIGURE THIS...

...OUT...

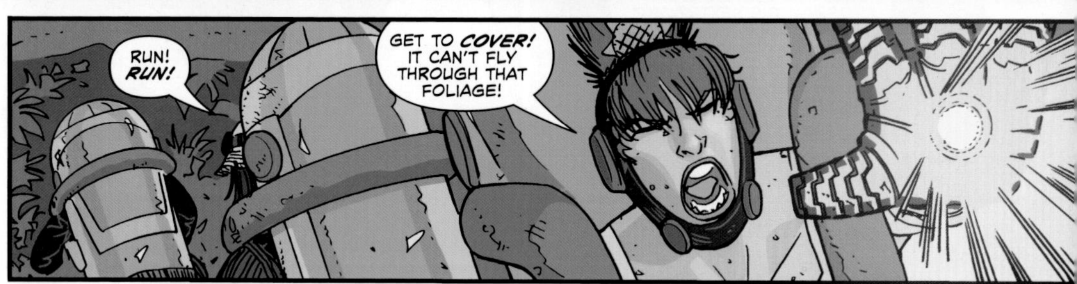
RUN! RUN!
GET TO COVER! IT CAN'T FLY THROUGH THAT FOLIAGE!

WE HAVE TO RECONNECT TO GET OUT OF HERE!

HURRY!

NOT TOO FAST!
FASTER, HERB! FASTER!
CLIK CLIK CLIK

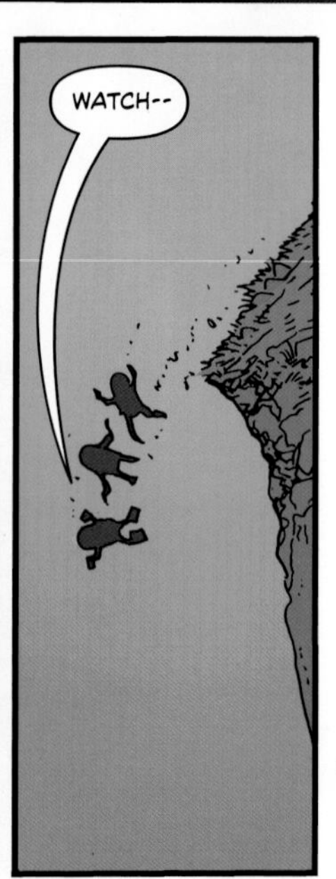
WATCH--

--OUT
ZZZZIF

Nnng!
NnNF!
UnGh!

BLARG!
ARE YOU SURE WE'RE GOING FORWARD IN TIME, HERB?
YES, YES. HUMANITY'S EGO LETS US THINK WE ARE POWERFUL ENOUGH TO DESTROY THE EARTH, BUT IN REALITY-- THE EARTH HAS GONE THROUGH COUNTLESS CYCLES OF BIRTH AND REBIRTH.
THOUSANDS OF ATOMIC CATASTROPHES AND ECOLOGICAL DISASTERS FOLLOWED BY ERAS OF RECOVERY. AS A RESULT, MANY FUTURE ERAS WILL PROBABLY SEEM EVEN MORE...

...PRIMITIVE...

...OR...

...BARBARIC...

WHAT ARE YOU *WAITING FOR,* HERB? JUMP US *NOW!*

I CAN'T...IT TAKES A FEW MINUTES FOR THE PACK TO RECHARGE. IT'S RUNNING ON A COMPLEX SYSTEM OF SOLAR, RADIATION, AND PERPETUAL MOTION SYSTEMS THAT ARE ACTUALLY QUITE CLEVER IN THAT THEY UTILIZE OUR FUTURE POSSIBILITIES AND PAST ACTIONS TO--
HERB--

--*SHUT UP* FOR A MINUTE.

LOOKS LIKE *THIS IS IT.* HONESTLY, NOT FAR OFF FROM HOW I *PICTURED* US GOING OUT.

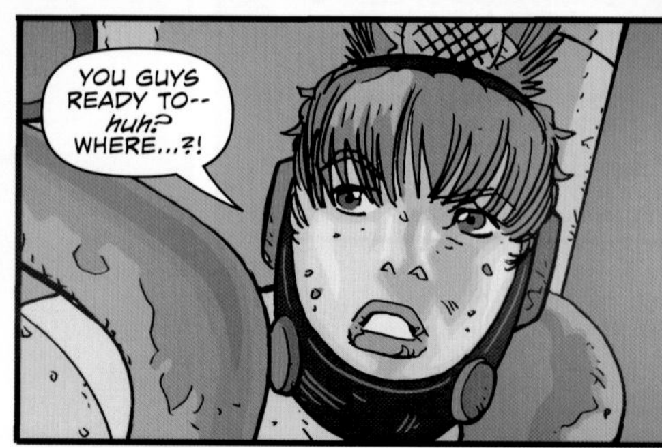

YOU GUYS READY TO-- *huh?* WHERE...?!

RUN, MARGE!
YOU #@#& #&%@S!
BOOM
BRASH
CRAK
BLAM
THIS WAY TO HIGHER GROUND! WE ONLY NEED ANOTHER MINUTE!
UN... UNBELIEVABLE...
DAMMIT. PACK GOT HIT BY A STRAY ROUND. GOING TO TAKE ME A FEW MORE MINUTES TO TEST THE SYSTEMS... JUST SIT TIGHT.

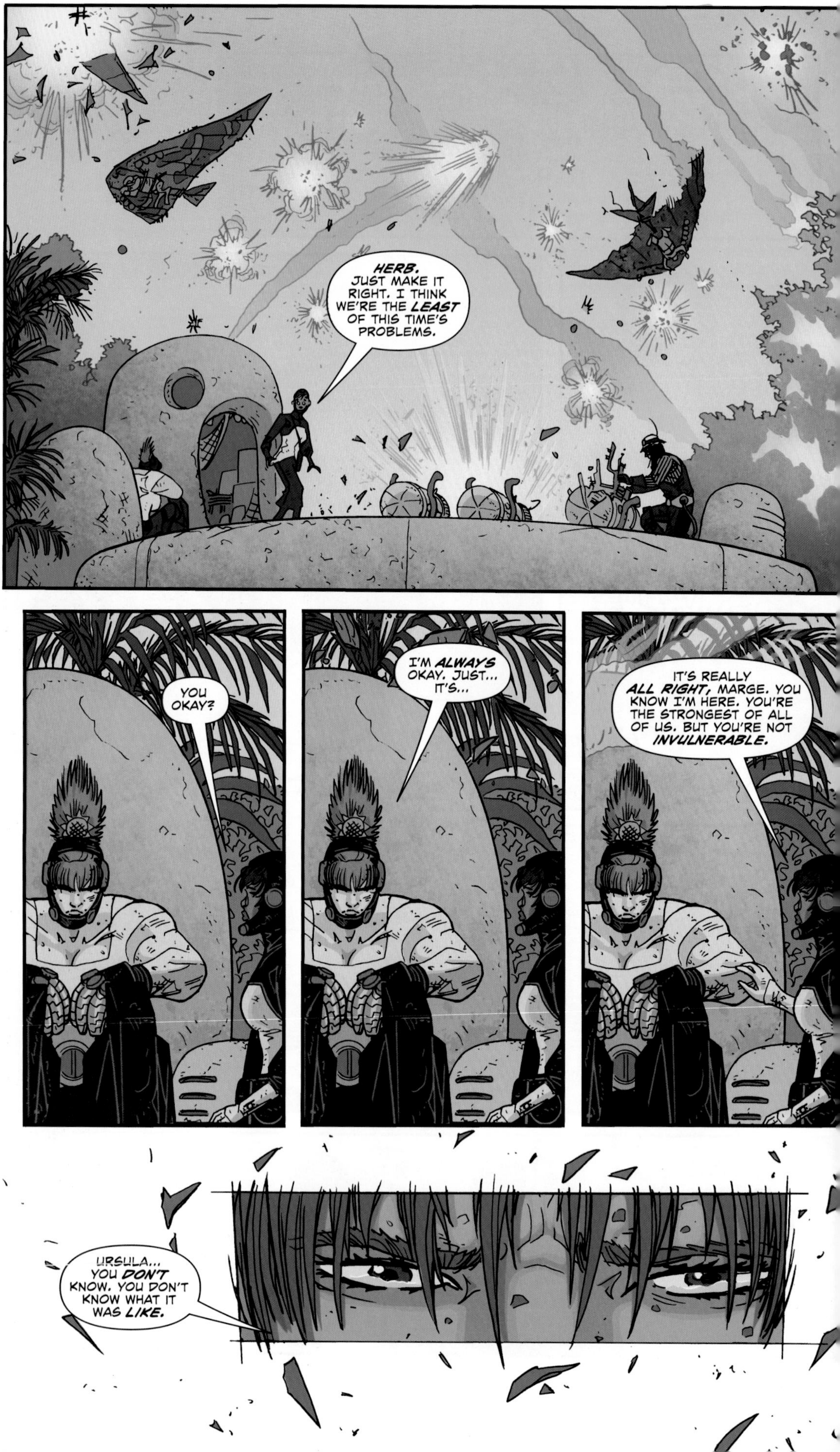

HERB. JUST MAKE IT RIGHT. I THINK WE'RE THE LEAST OF THIS TIME'S PROBLEMS.

YOU OKAY?

I'M ALWAYS OKAY. JUST... IT'S...

IT'S REALLY ALL RIGHT, MARGE. YOU KNOW I'M HERE. YOU'RE THE STRONGEST OF ALL OF US. BUT YOU'RE NOT INVULNERABLE.

URSULA... YOU DON'T KNOW. YOU DON'T KNOW WHAT IT WAS LIKE.

"MY TRAINING WAS **MORE**
TENSE THAN YOU COULD KNOW.
HE MONKS WERE FEARED ALL
OVER THE GALAXY.

"THE **TRIALS** WE HAD TO PASS, JUST TO BECOME THE **LOWEST GRUNTS,** WERE MORE THAN **ANYTHING** YOU COULD IMAGINE.

WE WERE TRAINED TO BE THE MOST UNFEELING, **OUGHEST** COMBATANTS IN RECORDED HISTORY.

"THE UNITED GALAXIES DEPLOYED US **CONSTANTLY...**

"ALWAYS INTO THE MOST HAZARDOUS SITUATIONS. WE FACED... **THINGS...** THAT YOU WOULD NEVER **BELIEVE.**

"THE **LAST** MISSION I WENT ON...WE WERE SENT TO CLEAR A PLANET FOR A MINING OPERATION. IT WAS INFESTED WITH MIND-LEACHING ALIENS. THEY MADE IT **UNINHABITABLE.**

"WE WERE SENT IN TO EXTERMINATE THEM.
"ALL AROUND ME, MY FELLOW MONKS WERE DOING THEIR JOB.
"MAKING THE PLANET SAFE FOR HUMANS TO EXPLOIT.
"THE MIND LEACHES EXPLOITED EMOTIONS. SPECIFICALLY HUMAN COMPASSION. EMPATHY. THEY FED OFF OF IT.
"NEEDLESS TO SAY, WHEN WE LANDED, THEY DIDN'T GET MUCH TO EAT."
GET IN THE FIGHT! THIS IS WHAT WE TRAINED YOU FOR, YOU SPINELESS %!$&@!

"I DON'T KNOW WHAT IT WAS THAT LAST TIME.
"I'D PASSED ALL OF THE MONKS' TRIALS. DONE THINGS FAR MORE BRUTAL THAN CRUSHING SOME HELPLESS SLIME MOLDS.
"I JUST DON'T KNOW.
"MAYBE IT WAS THE SLIME FEEDING ON MY EMPATHY.
"OR MAYBE I WAS JUST @$&% TIRED OF BEING TOLD TO BLINDLY FOLLOW ORDERS."

THEY KICKED ME OUT OF THE ORDER AFTER THAT. DISGRACED. DISOWNED. THIS MISSION. *OUR* MISSION? IT IS...*WAS* EVERYTHING. GETTING HOME DOESN'T MATTER TO ME NOW. THERE'S NOTHING THERE. I DON'T *NEED* IT.

AND I DON'T *NEED* WHATEVER YOU'RE OFFERING, URSULA. I DON'T NEED A COMPANION. I DON'T NEED A HELPING HAND. I *KNOW* WHO I AM AND WHAT I'M ABOUT.

MARGE. YOU KNOW I WAS TRAINED FOR THIS TEAM. TO REPLACE *ANYONE.* I'M THE BACKUP. THE FILL-IN. I'M TRAINED IN SCIENCE. I HAVE LEADERSHIP ABILITIES. IF *ANY ONE* OF US WAS LOST, I COULD FILL THE SPOT.

EXCEPT *YOU.* YOU WEREN'T REPLACEABL OF ALL THE CANDIDAT AND ALL THE TRAININ THEY COULD TRAIN M AND PREPARE ME TO ALL OF MY TEAMMATE JOBS. BUT *NO ONE* WAS ABLE TO REPLICA *YOUR* ROLE.
YEAH? WHAT *IS* MY ROLE, URSULA?

IT'S READY! *LET'S GO!*

JUST A *FEW MORE* JUMPS AND WE SHOULD *BE THERE...*
CLIK
CLIK
CLIK

CLIK

ZZZIIIFFFF

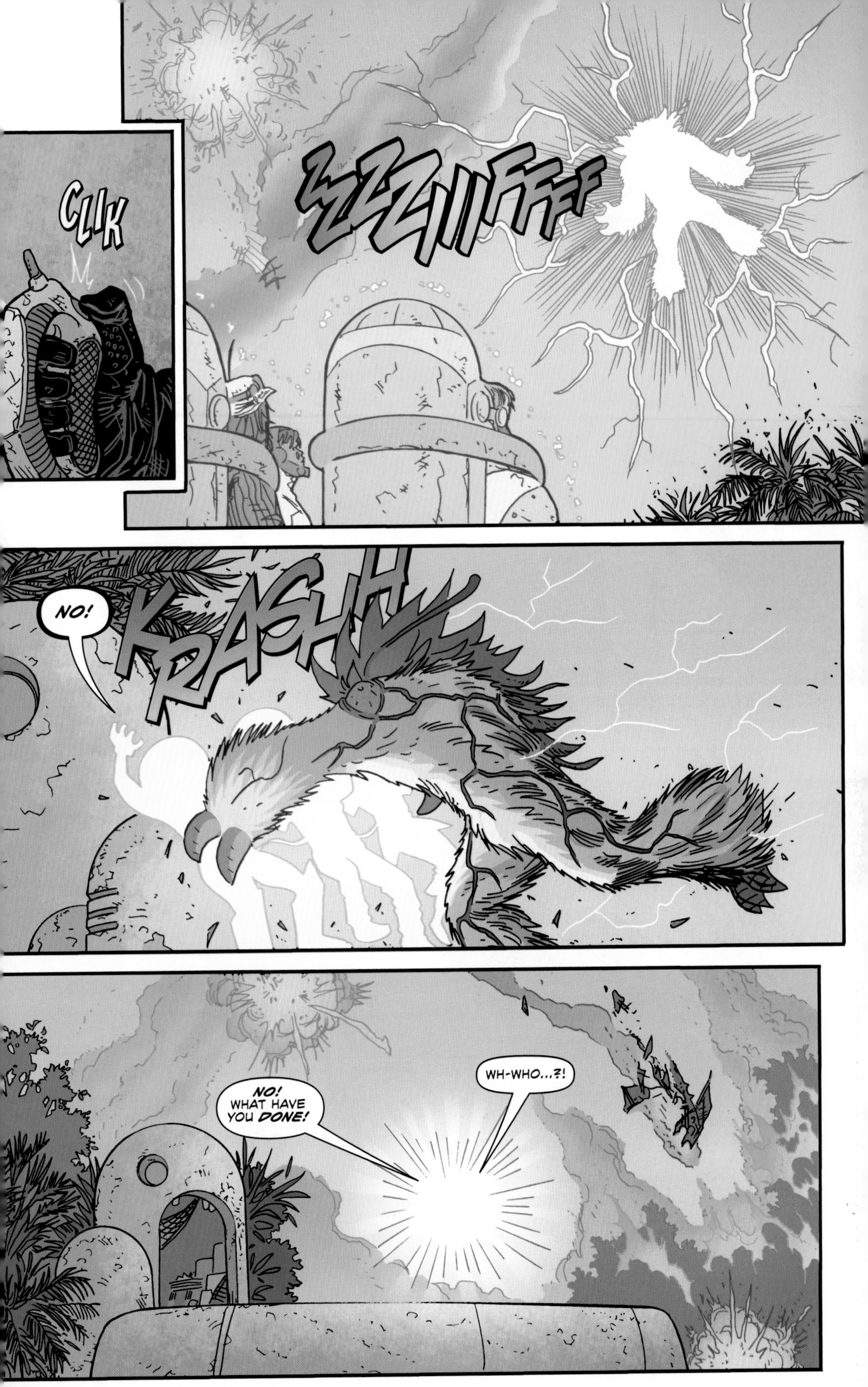

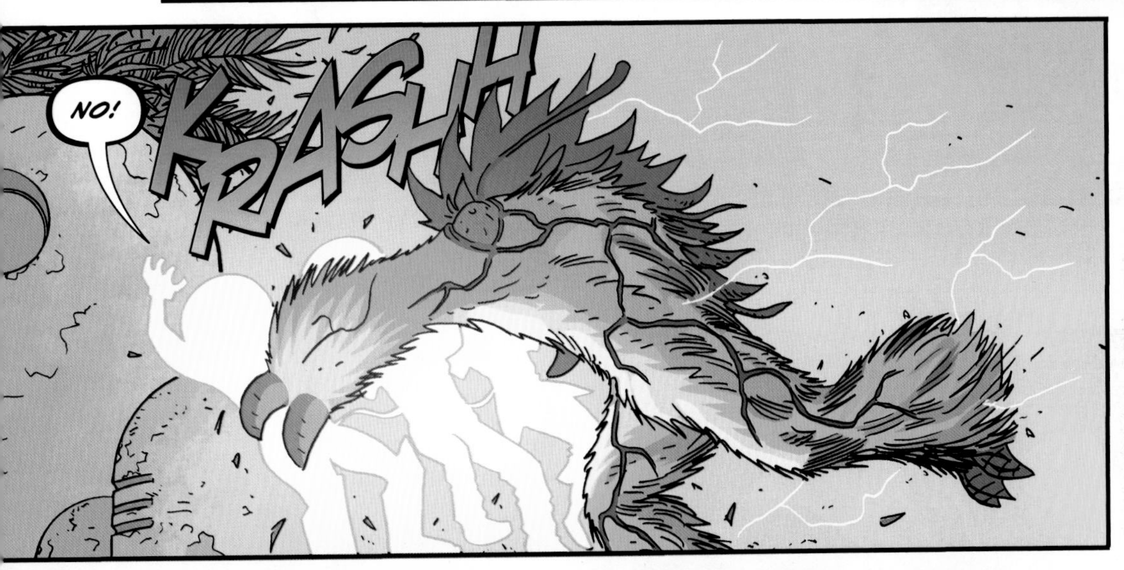
NO!
KRASHH

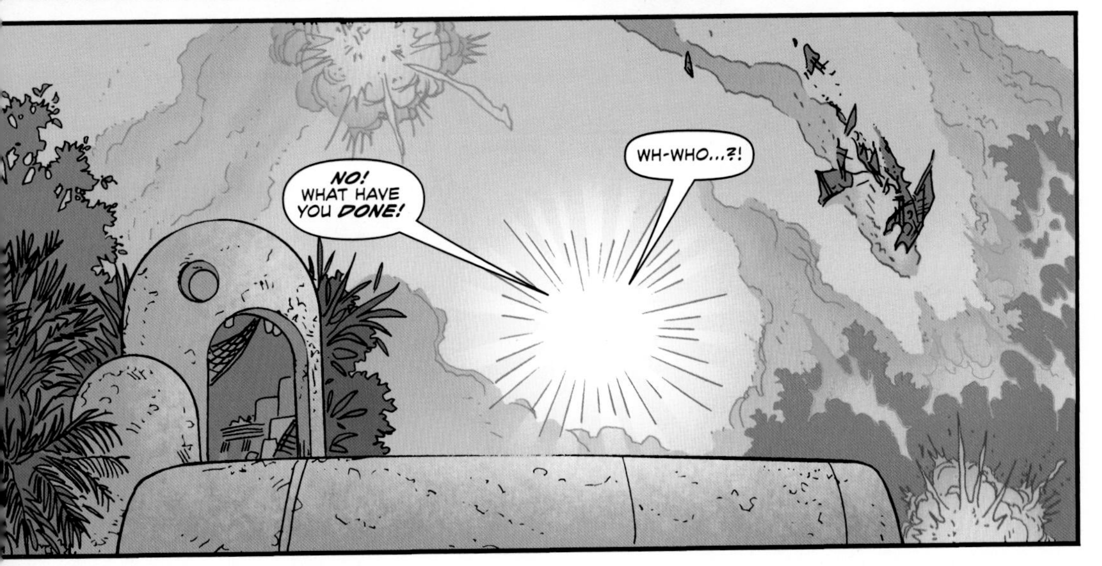
NO! WHAT HAVE YOU **DONE!**
WH-WHO...?!

WHAT THE HELL?!
4358* ()R5()74*45RG3* MU57 D13!!!!
PHIL?!

HERBERT JUNE TRAVELOGUE (excerpt)

December 2015.

Today, for the first time in my life, I moved with purpose but with no tangible goal . . . for the sake of the movement alone. And for the first time since we have been stranded here, I truly felt the barbaric nature of this ancient era.

But let me back up a bit. Having been here nearly a year (in ancient-calendar days), I have purposefully immersed myself in the culture, the customs, and the cuisine of this time. I partook in all manner of entertainment, diversions, and cuisine that are both typical of and ubiquitous in my new surroundings.

As a result, I had imbibed every manner of crudely brewed beverage and chemically enhanced "snack" food in hopes of better understanding the strangers in this strange land. And by degrees, I did slowly begin to understand the creatures of this era. What at first taste seemed bitter to me eventually became tolerable. And then desirable. The delectables that I found repulsively sweet on first encounter later became pleasurable to consume. In fact, I would often look forward to and anticipate the ingesting of sustenance, sheerly for the joy of the ingestion process.

What I failed to realize was that every ingestible item was chemically stunted. I was in fact poisoning myself with consumables that lacked the complex molecule burners that react inside our bodies to maximize caloric exploitation and eliminate excess nutritional intake. This eventually sent my body into a veritable tailspin as it rushed to cope with provisions that seem to have been genetically modified by imbecilic Cro-Magnon men intent on destroying themselves.

So this month I found myself having to manually override my body's calorie-utilization systems and perform pointless "exercises" in an effort to bring my body back to its optimum weight and density. Truly barbaric times.

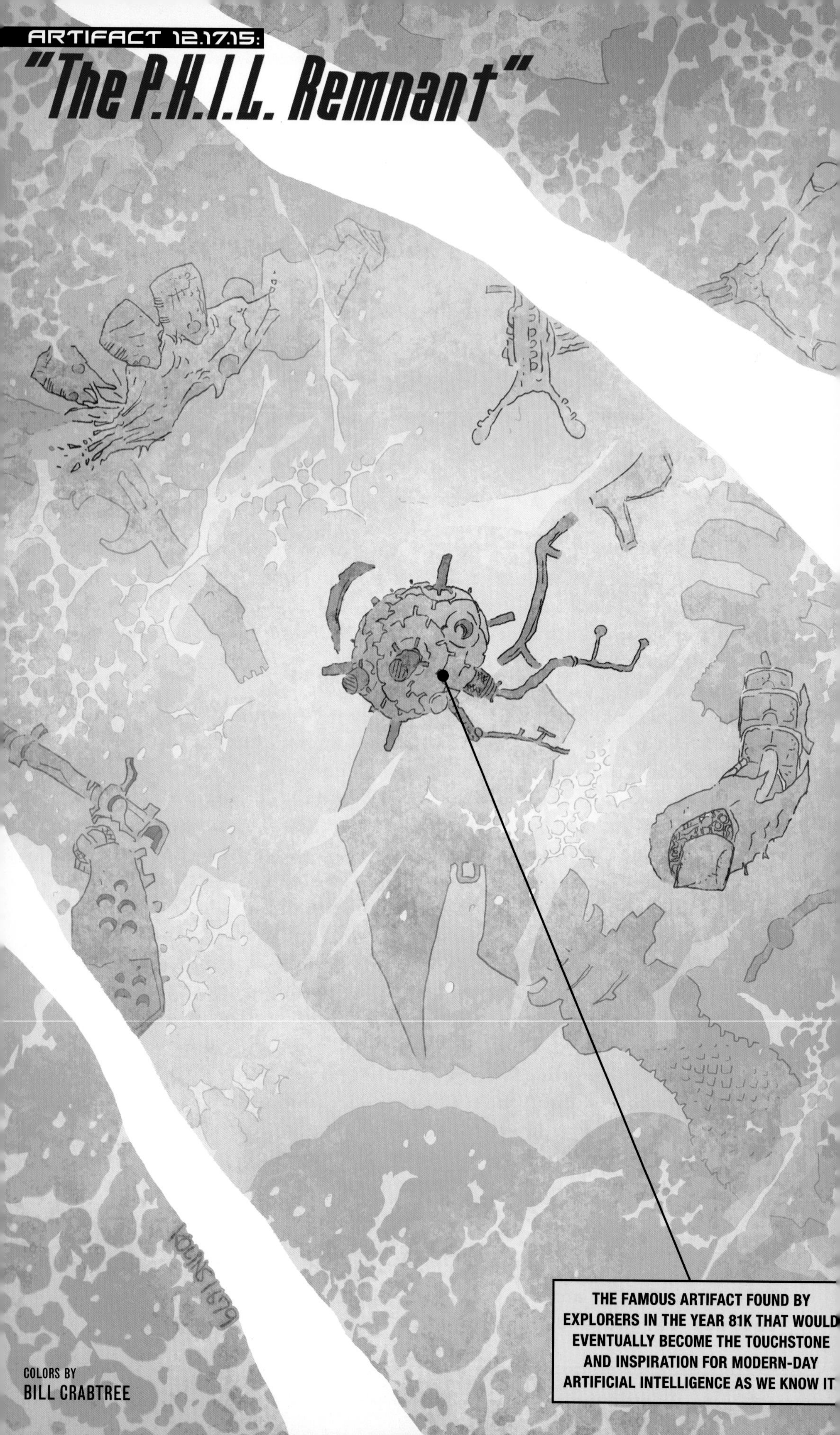
ARTIFACT 12.17.15:
"The P.H.I.L. Remnant"
THE FAMOUS ARTIFACT FOUND BY EXPLORERS IN THE YEAR 81K THAT WOULD EVENTUALLY BECOME THE TOUCHSTONE AND INSPIRATION FOR MODERN-DAY ARTIFICIAL INTELLIGENCE AS WE KNOW IT
COLORS BY
BILL CRABTREE

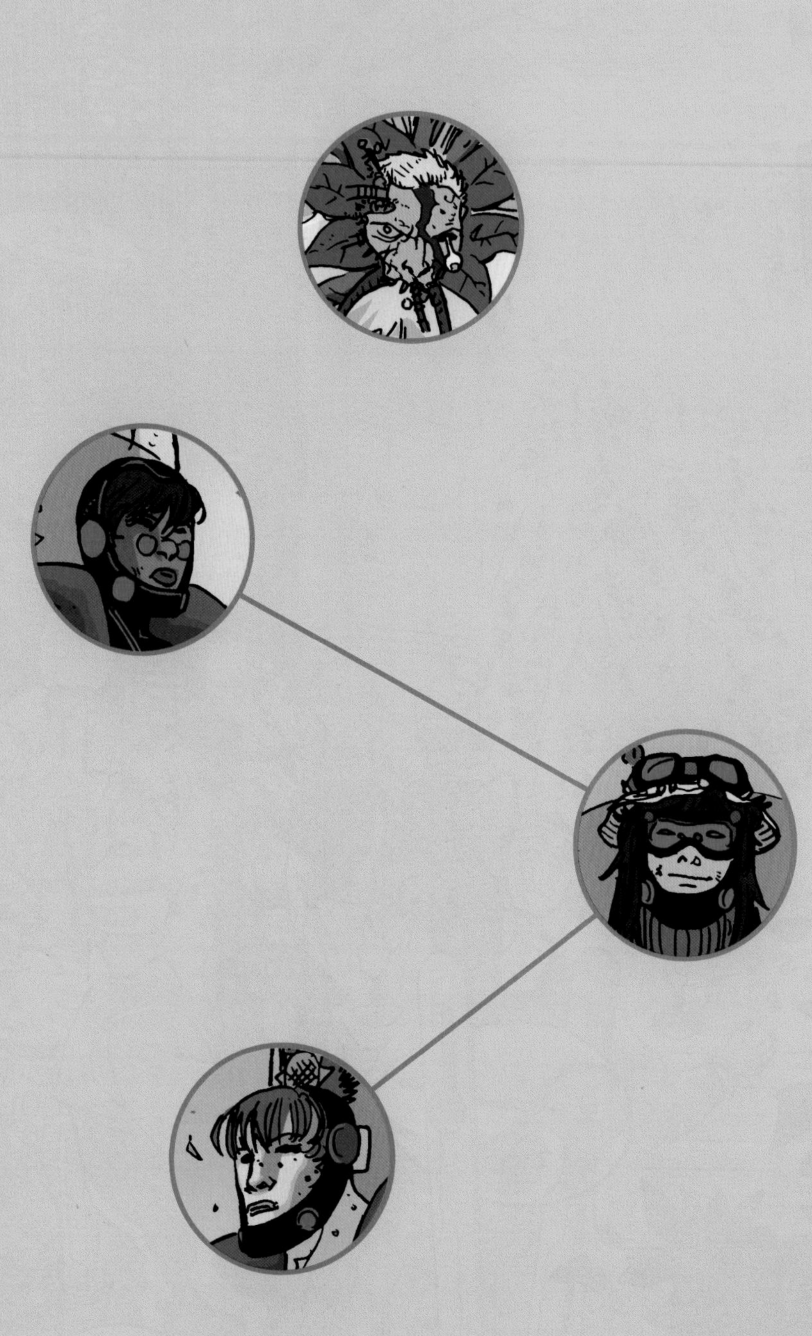

KOLINS 1999

PAST AWAYS™
MATT KINDT SCOTT KOLINS BILL CRABTREE

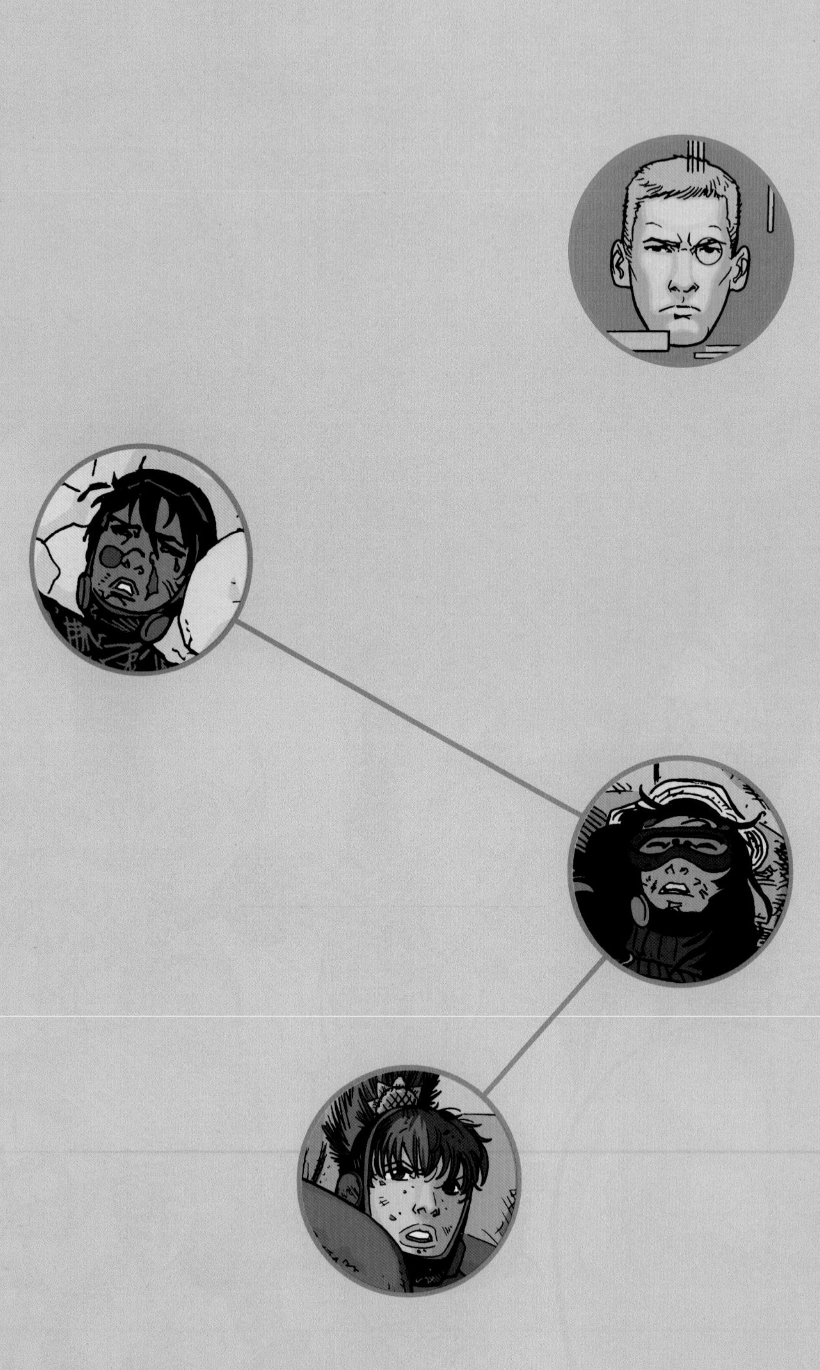

The Pseudo-Slums Hi-Rise Apartments.

WE'RE CLOSE TO GETTING BACK HOME. BY MY RECKONING, WE'RE ONLY ABOUT TEN THOUSAND YEARS FROM OUR TIME. ONE MORE JUMP SHOULD DO IT. AS FOR YOUR SECOND QUESTION...

HERE IT COMES!
IT LOOKS LIKE ONE OF THE CREATUR FROM ARTHUR'S TRO ROOM. BUT THERE'S SOMETHING STRANG ABOUT IT...

SOMETHING IS GRAFTED ON TO IT... LOOKS LIKE... LIKE...

NO. NO. ***NO!*** WE HAVE TO GET OUT OF--

KRNCSHHH

YOU DID A BAD THING. YOU ALL DID A BAD THING.

BZADYKYKYK
OOF!
I AM THE FATHER OF TIME! I AM THE PROGENITOR OF A PERFECT WAY OF THINKING!
NO...ghhk! PHIL... YOU'RE CRAZY. YOU'RE FROM A BILLION YEARS IN THE FUTURE. YOU CAN'T BE THE ORIGIN OF YOUR OWN TECHNOLOGY.
YOU ARE A HERETIC, HERBERT! AND I...I AM A GOD!
WELL... TECHNICALLY YOU'RE GRAFTED TO AN ULTRAMODERN PSEUDOGOD...

...Gasp BUT YOU'RE NOT...nGHhh... FAR OFF, PHIL.
NO!
GET OFF OF HIM!
Portable charge dispensers ideal for recharging critical electronic equipment and stunning psychotic automatons grafted to mythic alien beasts.

HE'S DISABLED! YOU'RE GONNA BE OKAY, HERB... YOU'RE...
...Nghhh...
UH-OH.
...NO...

CRANCHHHHH

BRSHHHHH

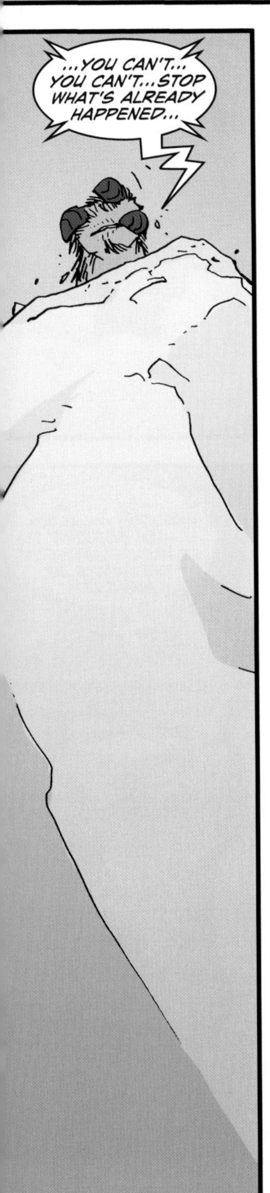
...YOU CAN'T... YOU CAN'T...STOP WHAT'S ALREADY HAPPENED...

...YOUR MINDS AREN'T DESIGNED TO PROCESS THE ULTRACONCEPTS I'VE DEVELOPED...

...YOU'RE NOTHING BUT APES DRAWING IN DIRT WITH YOUR FINGERS...

WH-WHAT HAPPENED TO YOU, PHIL? YOU KILLED ART. H-HE SAVED YOU, DIDN'T HE?
YOU OWED HIM. IF NOT...nghh... IF NOT US...AT LEAST HIM.

...NGha? WHAT? YES... YES...

WHEN I WAS WORKING ON MARS, I WAS SUBJECT TO YEARS OF ABUSE AT THE HANDS OF HUMANITY.

"ART DID
SAVE ME.
"HE SPARED NO EXPENSE TO BRING ME BACK TO FULL HEALTH.
"HE BEFRIENDED ME. HE OPENED UP TO ME. TOLD ME OF HIS PASSION FOR ADVENTURE. FOR TRAVEL. HIS CURIOSITY TO SEE THE UNKNOWN.
"HE LEFT ME TO RECHARGE ON HIS REHABILITATION EQUIPMENT. AND IT WAS THERE...AS I RECHARGED... AS I REGENERATED MY GRAY CELLS... THAT I TRULY AWOKE.
"AS I SAT IN THE DARK, I HAD WHAT I CAN ONLY DESCRIBE TO YOU AS A COSMIC EPIPHANY..."

ART KNEW MY PROGRAMMING BACKWARD AND FORWARD. HE KNEW THAT BY SAVING MY LIFE, MY INTERNAL LOGIC ROUTINES WOULD MAKE ME FEEL INDEBTED TO HIM FOR THE REST OF MY LIFE.

HE KNEW THAT MY PROGRAMMING WOULD FORCE ME TO FOLLOW HIM FOR THE REST OF MY DAYS, TRYING TO FULFILL MY LIFE DEBT TO HIM.

HIS INTENTIONS WEREN'T NOBLE...

HE KNEW...I WOULD BE HIS LIFELONG SERVANT. BUT SECRETLY HE FEARED ME. HE KNEW I WAS MEANT FOR SOMETHING MORE. HERE IN THE PAST I HAVE FOUND MY TRUE DESTINY. HE FEARED ME...BECAUSE I...I AM THE GOD OF FUTURE MAN! I AM--
YOU'RE DELUSION--

SHUT UP, URSULA.
BRZZZZAPP

WHA--?
CAREFUL, MARGE.
WE'RE WAY PAST CAREFUL, HERB.
BWARKKK
BZARK
CRASHHH

YOU KILLED URSULA, PHIL. ANY LAST WORDS, YOU MONSTER?!
FOOLS.

ZARKKK
CLUTCHING THE FEET OF GIANTS...

AGHH!

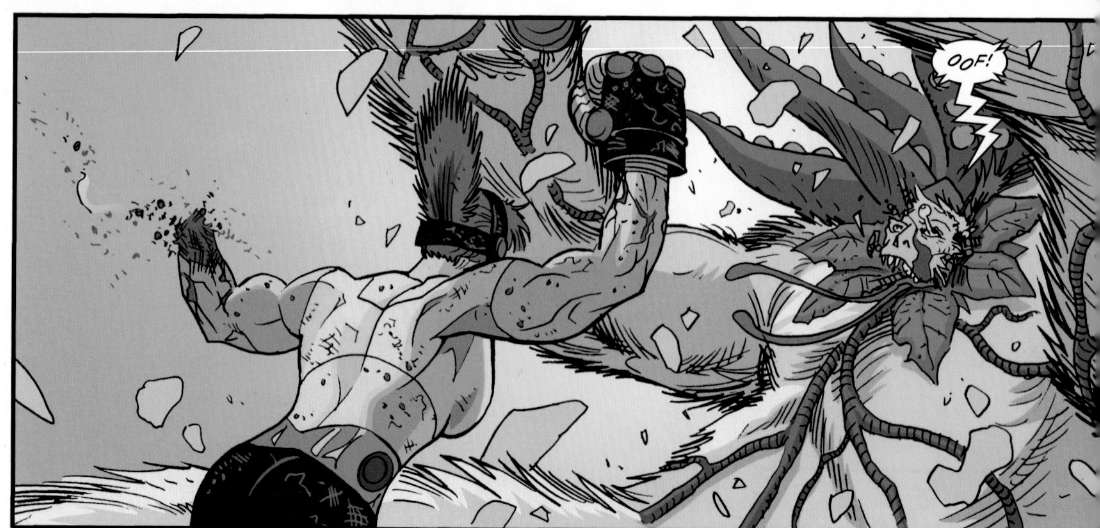
OOF!

DIE, PHIL!
DIE...!
...I BECOME... I BECAME... I AM...
...DEATH... THE BRINGER... OF GOD... I BECOME...
BRRAKKK
RENCHHH
CRNNCH
DIE!
DEAD.

ONE MORE JUMP, MARGE. WE'RE CLOSE ENOUGH NOW. THE TWO OF US CAN DO IT.

SEE YOU WHEN WE GET THERE.

□ The PHIL Remnant.

10,000 years later.

HERB. YOU EVER THINK IT'S STRANGE?
WHAT?
OUR MISSION.
WHAT DO YOU MEAN?

I MEAN...ME AND YOU. LAUNCHING THE TIME TECH WITHOUT PERMISSION. HEADING BILLIONS OF YEARS INTO THE PAST.
I REMEMBER DOING IT. SO...NO. NOT WEIRD. IT WAS ALL MY FAULT, MARGE. I HIT THE BUTTON. WE WEREN'T APPROVED FOR THE MISSION BUT I WANTED TO GO SO BAD. MY FAMILY DIED. I WANTED TO UNDO IT.

NO, NO. IT'S NOT THAT. I GET THAT. IT'S JUST...WHY DID *WE* GO ALONE?
...
Most of us sink into the ocean...

DO YOU THINK IT'S STRANGE THAT THEY WOULD ONLY SEND US? JUST TWO AGENTS? NO BACKUP. NO REDUNDANCY?
YEAH. I WONDERED ABOUT THAT TOO.
IT JUST SEEMS LIKE...
LIKE WE'RE FORGETTING SOMEONE.
But some of us skip across the surface for a little while.

WE'RE HEROES, MARGE. WE WENT SOMEWHERE. DID SOMETHING NO ONE ELSE HAS DONE. LET'S JUST TRY TO ENJOY IT. WE'LL ONLY BE ON THE NEWS VIDS FOR TWENTY SECONDS BEFORE THE NEXT BIG THING COMES ALONG.
Some of us longer than others...

But eventually we all sink.

The only trace of our existence is a memory that grows fainter over time.

A memory that melts away as we fade away.

Twenty seconds and one month later...

Those that knew
us fade away.

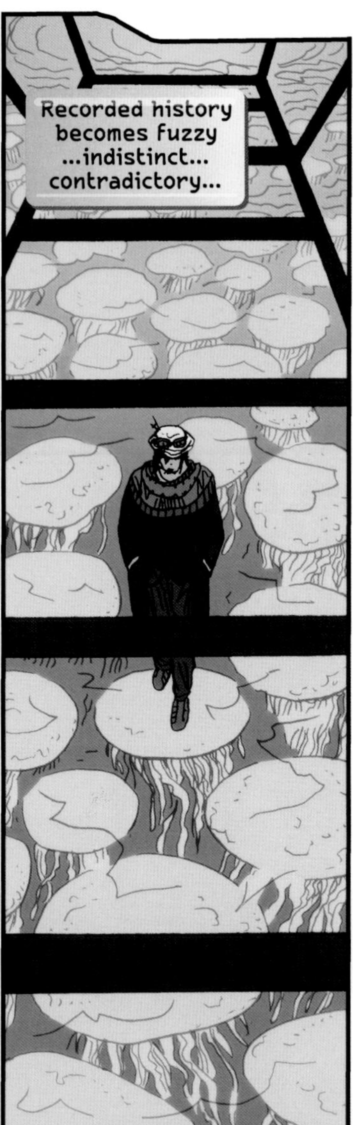
Recorded history
becomes fuzzy
...indistinct...
contradictory...

Until all that's
left is myth with
forgotten origins.

If we're lucky,
the myth is good
enough. A story
worth repeating.
Handed down.
Passed on.

Or past away.

I was obsessed with going backward. Did I think I could bring my family back?

But the only thing in the past is a lesson. A lesson to be learned.

You can't change what's happened. All you can do is take the lesson...

And move forward.

I'LL HAVE NUMBER SEVENTY-TWO.

IS THIS... IS THIS COFFEE?!
WHAT ELSE WOULD IT BE?

THANK YOU.

☐ Coffee: vintage archaeology-salvaged fold-gers beans handpicked by scavenger Earth monkeys.